THEMATIC UNIT
Silkworms and Mealworms

Written by Sarah Kartchner Clark, M.A.

Teacher Created Materials, Inc.
6421 Industry Way
Westminster, CA 92683
www.teachercreated.com
©1999 Teacher Created Materials, Inc.
Reprinted, 2000
Made in U.S.A.
ISBN-1-57690-371-0

Illustrator
Ken Tunell

Editor
Janet A. Hale, M.S. Ed.

Cover Artist
Agi Palinay

The classroom teacher may reproduce copies of materials in this book for classroom use only. The reproduction of any part for an entire school or school system is strictly prohibited. No part of this publication may be transmitted, stored, or recorded in any form without written permission from the publisher.

Table of Contents

Introduction 3

Silkworms by Sylvia Johnson (Lerner Publications Co., 1982) 5
   (Available in Canada, Riverwood Pub.; UK, Turnaround; AUS, Stafford Bks.)

   Summary—Sample Plan—Overview of Activities—Silkworm Instructions—Silkworms Discussion Questions—Domesticated Animals—Metamorphosis Cycle—Unscramble the Words—Through the Eyes of a Silkworm

The Empress and the Silkworm by Lily Toy Hong (Albert Whitman & Co., 1995) 16
   (Available in Canada, General Pub.; UK, Baker & Taylor; AUS, Stafford Bks.)

   Summary—Sample Plan—Overview of Activities—Story Sequence—How Silk is Made—Compounded Animals—Silkworm Sentences

My Mealworm Book (A Make-It-Yourself Book) 24

   Summary—Sample Plan—Overview of Activities—Mealworm Instructions—My Mealworm Book Overview—My Mealworm Book—Look at the Mealworm!—How Do Mealworms Walk?—How Do Mealworms Find Bran?—What Do Mealworms Eat?—Mealworms and Apples—Mealworm Maze—A Mealworm's Favorite Color—Favorite Color Data Sheet—Magnificent Mealworms

Across the Curriculum 45

    Language Arts: Journal Entry Questions—Journal Cover—Create-a-Sentence—Poetry Page—A Day in the Life of a Silkworm

    Math: Silkworm Scavenger Hunt—Place Value Practice—Mealworm Mania

    Science: Beetle Mania—What am I? Riddles—What is a Worm?—How Strong is Silk?

    Social Studies: Producers of Silk Map—Some Creepy Crawlies Help Us

    Art: See-a-Scene—Spin a Cocoon—Creepy Crawly Mealworm

    Drama: Popsicle Puppets

    Music: Wormy Musical Songs

    Life Skills: Cooking with Bran (A Take-Home Sheet)

Culminating Activity 67
   Culmination Games—Show What You Know

Unit Management 69
   Silkworm and Mealworm Habitats—Silkworm and Mealworm Vocabulary—Letters to Parents—Bulletin Boards—Learning Centers—Door Invitations—Classroom Door Activities—Behavioral Management Ideas—Awards—Clip Art

Answer Key 79

Bibliography 80

Introduction

Silkworms and Mealworms contains a comprehensive whole-language, thematic unit. Its 80 reproducible pages are filled with a wide variety of lesson ideas and activities designed for use with young learners. At its core are two high-quality reading selections, and a create-your-own hands-on reading book.

There are activities for each literature selection which set the stage for reading, encourage the enjoyment of the book, and extend the concepts. Activities are also provided that integrate the curriculum areas of language arts, math, science, social studies, art, music, and life skills. Many of the activities are conducive to the use of cooperative learning groups.

Unit Management tools include time-saving suggestions, such as patterns for bulletin boards and learning centers.

This thematic unit includes:

- **literature selections**—summaries of two children's books with related lessons that cross the curriculum

- **planning guides**—suggestions for introducing the unit, sequencing the lessons, and making projects and displays

- **curriculum connections**—activities in language arts, math, science, social studies, art, music, physical education, and life skills that you can incorporate into your daily curriculum

- **unit management suggestions**—teacher aids for organizing the unit, including incentives, patterns, and a unit award

- **culminating activity**—class activity that will enrich the classroom experience and synthesize the learning

- **bibliography**—suggested additional readings relating to the theme

---

To keep this valuable resource intact so that it can be used year after year, you may wish to punch holes in the pages and store them in a three-ring binder.

Introduction (cont.)

Why a Balanced Approach?

The strength of a whole language approach is that it involves children in using all modes of communication—reading, writing, listening, illustrating, and doing. Communication skills are interconnected and integrated into lessons that emphasize the whole of language. Balancing this approach is our knowledge that every whole—including individual words—is composed of parts, and directed study of those parts can help a student to master the whole. Experience and research tell us that regular attention to phonics, other word attack skills, spelling, etc., develops reading mastery, thereby fulfilling the unity of the whole language experience. The child is thus led to read, write, spell, speak, and listen confidently in response to a literature experience introduced by the teacher. In these ways, language skills grow rapidly, stimulated by direct practice, involvement, and interest in the topic at hand.

Why Thematic Planning?

One very useful tool for implementing a balanced language program is thematic planning. By choosing a theme with correlating literature selections for a unit of study, a teacher can plan activities throughout the day that lead to a cohesive, in-depth study of the topic. Students will be practicing and applying their skills in meaningful contexts. Consequently, they tend to learn and retain more. Both teachers and students will be freed from a day that is broken into unrelated segments of isolated drill and practice.

Why Cooperative Learning?

Besides academic skills and content, students need to learn social skills. This area of development cannot be taken for granted. Students must learn to work cooperatively in groups in order to function well in modern society. Group activities should be a regular part of school life, and teachers should consciously include social objectives as well as academic objectives in their planning. For example, a group working together to solve a problem may need to select a leader. Teachers should make clear to the students the qualities of good leader-follower group interaction just as they would state and monitor the academic goals of the project.

Four Basic Components of Cooperative Learning

1. In cooperative learning, all group members need to work together to accomplish the task.
2. Cooperative learning groups should be heterogeneous.
3. Cooperative learning activities need to be designed so that each student contributes to the group, and individual group members can be assessed on their performance.
4. Cooperative learning teams need to know the social as well as the academic objectives of a lesson.

Silkworms

by Sylvia Johnson

Summary

Have you ever wondered what a silkworm is? It isn't really a worm! It is the caterpillar of the silkworm moth. **Silkworms**, *an award winning nonfictional book, gives all the information needed to learn the basics of the silkworm in an easy-to-read format.* **Silkworms** *explains the life cycle of a silkworm moth, labels the parts of a silkworm, and gives detailed information on how a silkworm spins silk.*

This book can be used to teach the information on the silkworm and can also be used as a resource in a classroom reference library. It is filled with colorful illustrations to give students a close-up view of the life of a silkworm.

Sample Plan

Lesson 1
- Set up The Silkworm Story Bulletin Board (page 72) and True or False Learning Center (page 74).
- Do KWL activity (page 6, #6).
- Review Silkworm Instructions (page 9).
- Make silkworm habitats (page 69).
- Discuss silkworm vocabulary (page 14).
- Read pages 5–13 of *Silkworms* as a class.
- Do Stage 1 discussion questions (page 10).
- Make journals (page 45).
- Discuss domesticated animals. Complete the activity on page 12.
- Complete Silkworm Scavenger Hunt activity (page 50).

Lesson 2
- Read pages 14–23 of *Silkworms* as a class.
- Complete Stage 2 discussion questions (page 10).
- Complete a daily journal question (page 45).
- Do Metamorphosis Cycle activity (page 13).
- Make cocoons and tissue paper moths (page 61).

Lesson 3
- Read pages 24–37 of *Silkworms* as a class.
- Complete Stage 3 discussion questions (page 11).
- Review metamorphosis with What Am I? Riddles (page 54).
- Learn about animals eyes using Through the Eyes of a Silkworm (page 15).

Lesson 4
- Read pages 38–45 of *Silkworms* as a class.
- Complete Stage 4 discussion questions (page 11).
- Complete a daily journal question (page 45).
- Distinguish between a worm and a caterpillar. Have children complete What is a Worm? (page 55).
- Complete the culminating activities on page 67.

Silkworms

Overview of Activities

Setting the Stage

1. Assemble The Silkworm Story Bulletin Board (page 72) and the True or False Learning Center (page 74).

2. Copy the first parent letter (page 71) about the upcoming unit of study on silkworms and mealworms. Send the letters home with the children on the first day of the unit.

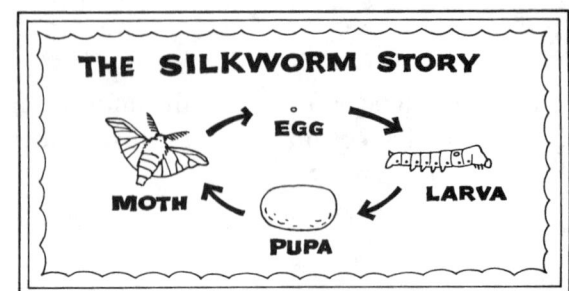

3. Review the teacher information (page 9) about the silkworm and the instructions on caring for silkworms.

4. Assemble writing journals as directed on page 45.

5. Assemble silkworm habitats for each child (page 69). Using one of the silkworm habitats, gather the children around in a semi-circle. Place a silkworm in your hand and ask the children what it is. Allow thoughts, feelings, ideas, and suggestions to come from each child. Ask the children to describe the silkworm. What do they think it is called? What does it eat? What does it do? Explain to the children that they will be studying these silkworms over the next few weeks.

6. On a large piece of butcher paper, write the words *Know*, *Want to Know*, and *Learned*, across the top. Have the children turn to the first page in their journals and write these same words across the top. Ask the children to write down all the things they know about silkworms under the word *Know* and all the things they want to know under the *Want To Know* column. Then gather together in a group and have the children share all the things they know and want to know about silkworms. Record the responses on the butcher paper. Display this in a prominent place in the classroom so that as learning occurs new knowledge can be recorded under the *Learned* column. When you have finished your lessons, make reference to this chart to help children clarify and cement their learning. This is called a KWL Chart.

Enjoying the Book

1. Gather the children in a semi-circle on the floor so all can see the book title. Spend a few minutes as a class discussing this new book. Have children look at the title. Who wrote the book? Who did the pictures? What might the story be about? Have you ever read a story about a worm? Tell students that this book is about a worm-like creature called a silkworm.

Silkworms

Overview of Activities *(cont.)*

Enjoying the Book *(cont.)*

2. Ask discussion questions daily (page 10). This will help you teach the concepts of the silkworm. Allow "wait time" between questions to ensure that all children have had a chance to think about their answers.

3. In the story *Silkworms*, the author talks about the fact that silkworms are domesticated animals. Discuss with students what domesticated and wild animals are. After discussing the difference between the two, complete the Domesticated Animals activity on page 12.

4. Enjoy the Silkworm Scavenger Hunt activity (page 50) so the children can become more familiar with the size, weight, and color of a silkworm.

5. *Silkworms* is a great resource to learn about the life cycle of a silkworm. Provide each child with a live silkworm to observe as it ventures through its life cycle. You may purchase silkworm eggs or you may purchase silkworms larvae (see *Insect Lore*, page 80). Have the children put their silkworms in their silkworm habitats (page 69). Make the Life Cycle Door Invitation (page 75). Track the progress of each child's silkworm. Children should be keeping a daily account in their journals of their silkworm's progress. Use page 13 to share knowledge about the stages of metamorphosis.

6. Make a 3-D model of a silkworm cocoon and a tissue paper moth (page 61). This art activity is easy to do and makes an impressive visual display in your classroom.

7. Review the vocabulary words on page 14. The life cycle words need to be unscrambled. This activity can be done as an entire class, in small groups, or as an individual assignment.

8. Another review of the silkworm metamorphosis is the What am I? Riddles activity on page 54. Children will enjoy making up riddles of their own at the end of this activity.

9. Doing the Through the Eyes of a Silkworm activity (page 15) will give children a first-eye view of what it is like to see differently. After children have experimented with each of the eye centers, ask them these questions: What did it feel like to see this way? What would be difficult to do if this was how you could see? (As an extension, invite a blind person to come and talk to your class about the challenges of not being able to see at all or just being able to see blurry images. What tools does he or she use to make life easier? What things does he or she need to change or adjust so he or she can live safely?)

10. Play a game of Freeze Tag to simulate what a silkworm does between molts. A silkworm literally freezes (sleeps) while the skin is preparing to molt (shed its skin). Freeze Tag is played with a person being "It." This person tries to tag another player. If he or she is successful, then the player tagged freezes. This person cannot move until another player comes by to "unfreeze" (touch) the frozen player. "It" wins or is changed when all players have been frozen (are sleeping).

Silkworms

Overview of Activities (cont.)

Extending the Book

1. Read other books written by Sylvia Johnson. Discuss how they are alike and how they are different. Bring two Hula Hoops® to your classroom. Using index cards or square pieces of paper, have children write down or draw pictures of the similarities or differences. Then have students place their responses in the Hula Hoop® like a Venn diagram. (Each circle is for the differences. The section where in the Hula Hoops® intersect is for the similarities.)

2. Introduce Silky, the Silkworm (page 76) to the class. Explain your chosen behavioral program using Silky.

3. Teach children to distinguish the difference between a worm and a caterpillar. Complete the activity, What is a Worm? (page 55). Then read the book, *It Could Still be a Worm*, by Allan Fowler. Look at as many pictures of worms and caterpillars as you can find to solidify their understanding of the differences between the two creatures.

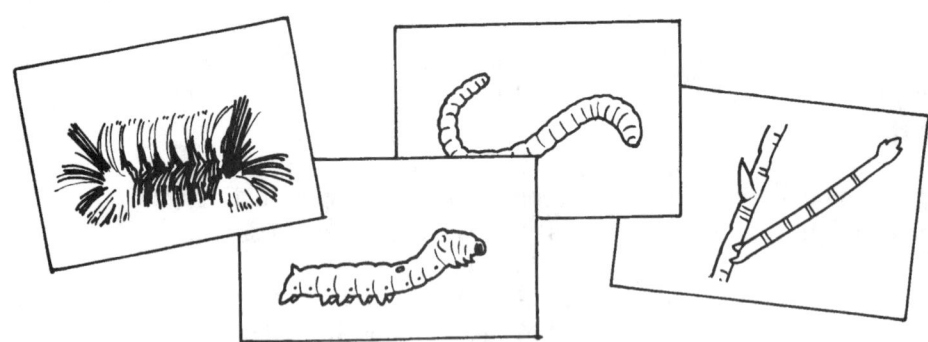

4. Check for understanding about silkworms by using the culminating word games found on page 67.

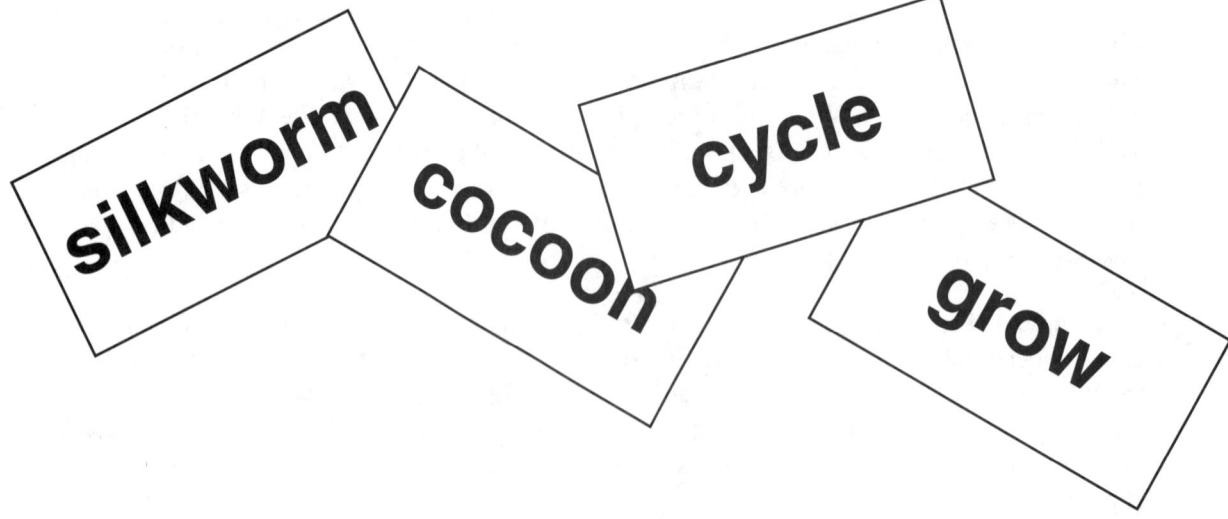

5. Have students complete the activity on page 23 as a review page for an assessment and to use as an evaluation tool.

Silkworm Instructions

This page will give you all the information you will need to know in order to successfully keep and raise silkworms in your classroom. Please read instructions carefully.

What are Silkworms?

Silkworms are not really worms. They are the larvae (or caterpillar) of the silkworm moth. Silkworms have become known for their silk cocoons. When unwound, these cocoons have strands of silk that can be woven into silk fabric. You can order silkworms through *Insect Lore* (page 80), as well as other insect distributors. You must have a ready supply of Mulberry leaves for the silkworm to eat. Check your local nurseries if Mulberry trees are not readily found in your area.

Life Cycle

Each female silkworm moth lays about 500 yellow eggs that are no larger than the size of the head of a pin. These eggs will grow from an egg to a larva (the silkworm), pupa, and finally become a silkworm moth. The silkworm moth only lives for a short time. It lives long enough to produce more of its kind.

Culturing Silkworms

To culture silkworms, use a plastic or glass container with smooth sides to prevent escape and to allow children to see the silkworm spin its cocoon. A wide-mouth gallon jar works well. Place the silkworms in the jar with mulberry leaves. Older mulberry leaves seem to work better. Do not put silkworms or their cocoons near water. This can kill them. Your children will have the opportunity to document each stage of the silkworm from egg to larva to pupa to silkworm moth. Save a few cocoons to unwind and talk about how silk is made.

Silkworms spend most of their time eating and eating and eating! In their larval form, silkworms will molt (lose their skin) four times. The periods before or after each molt are called instars. There are five instars in a silkworm's development:

INSTARS	1st	2nd	3rd	4th	5th
Days of eating and growth	2.5	2.5	3	4	8
Days of inactivity before molting	1	1	1.5	2	—

Silkworms

Silkworms Discussion Questions

As you read the book *Silkworms*, use the following critical thinking questions:

Stage 1—The Egg (pages 5-13)

- Is a silkworm a worm? (*No, it is a caterpillar.*)

- What does a silkworm turn into? (*silkworm moth*)

- Describe a silkworm moth. What does it look like? (*light color, furry body, feathery antennae*)

- Metamorphosis is a big word. What does it mean? (*a physical change some animals go through in its body structure or function*)

- What are domesticated animals? (*animals that need help from human beings to live*) Can you name a few? (*Answers will vary.*)

- Moths live for only a short time. How long do they live? (*a few days or weeks*)

- What is the silkworm moth's job? (*to make more silkworm moths*)

- Pheromones are chemical substances. What are they able to do with these? (*warn of danger, tell animals to stay away from each others' territories*)

- How big are the silkworm eggs? (*size of a pin head*)

- What color are the silkworm eggs? (*yellowish*)

Stage 2—Larva (pages 14-23)

- How do silkworms hatch from their eggs? (*by eating a hole in the soft covering of their egg*)

- What is a worm? (*a long, slender, soft-bodied creeping animal with no legs*) Teacher Note: Remember in the larva stage, a silkworm looks like a worm, but is actually a caterpillar.

- What do silkworms turn into? (*silkworm moths*)

- How long are the newly hatched silkworms? (*less than .118 inches [3 mm] long*)

- What do the new silkworms look like after they have hatched? (*They have black heads and bodies covered with hair.*)

- How long does it take for the silkworms to emerge from their eggs? (*approximately 20 days*)

- What do silkworms eat? (*mulberry leaves*)

- What is it called when the silkworm larva lose their skin? (*molting*)

- A silkworm will lose its skin five times. Right before a silkworm will molt it becomes very still like it is sleeping. These stages of molting and resting are called instars. How many instars does a silkworm go through? (*five*)

Silkworms Discussion Questions (cont.)

Stage 3—Pupa (pages 24–37)

- A silkworm's body has lots of parts. Ask the children what some of the parts of their bodies are. (*i.e. eyes, nose, ears, etc.*) Explain that a silkworm has 12 simple eyes. What is a simple eye? (*It can only tell the difference between light and dark.*)

- Other parts of a silkworm's body are the spinneret, trachae, malpighian tubes, spiracles, and silk glands. What do these parts do? (*Spinneret is a tube through which the silkworm sends out its silk; the trachae helps the silkworm breathe through the spiracles; the malpighian tubes eliminate waste, and the silk glands produce silk.*)

- Why does the silkworm spin silk? (*To form a cocoon.*)

- How are the silk spreads stuck together as they come out of the silkworm's body? (*With a sticky substance called sericin.*)

- A silkworm's cocoon is made up of one unbroken thread of silk. How long does it take for a silkworm to make a cocoon? (*At least two days.*)

- Inside the cocoon, the silkworm turns into what? (*The pupa.*)

- Unfortunately, if a person wants to use the cocoon for silk, it must destroy the pupa inside before it comes out. How does this happen? (*By putting the cocoons in a hot oven, or in boiling water, the pupa is killed.*) Teacher Note: Many people around the world then eat the pupa for food and nourishment.

Stage 4—The Silkworm Moth (pages 38–45)

- If the pupa is not destroyed, it will continue to change into a silkworm moth. How long will a pupa stay inside a cocoon? (*About three weeks.*)

- Show your children a picture of a silkworm and a picture of a silkworm moth. Let them talk about the differences. Does anything stay the same? What are some of the changes that a silkworm pupa goes through to turn into a moth? (*It gets longer hairy legs, its worm-like body turns into a short thick body covered with white scales, long feathery antennae, large compound eyes, and scaly white wings.*)

- How does a silkworm moth get out of its thick silky cocoon? (*It uses a special liquid that its body produces to soften and dissolve the silk.*)

- The last part the moth has to do is spread its wings. How long does it take for a new moth to do this? (*15 minutes.*)

- What is a silkworm moth's job once it has come out of the cocoon. (*Its job is to lay more eggs.*)

Silkworms

Domesticated Animals

Some animals are called wild animals. They feed and care for themselves. Other animals like your pet dog or cat need help from humans to live. These are called domesticated animals. We feed them and bathe them and care for them. A silkworm is also a domesticated animal and it needs help from humans to live.

1. Color all of the domesticated animals pictures.
2. Cut them out and paste them onto another piece of paper.
3. Try to write each domesticated animal's name.

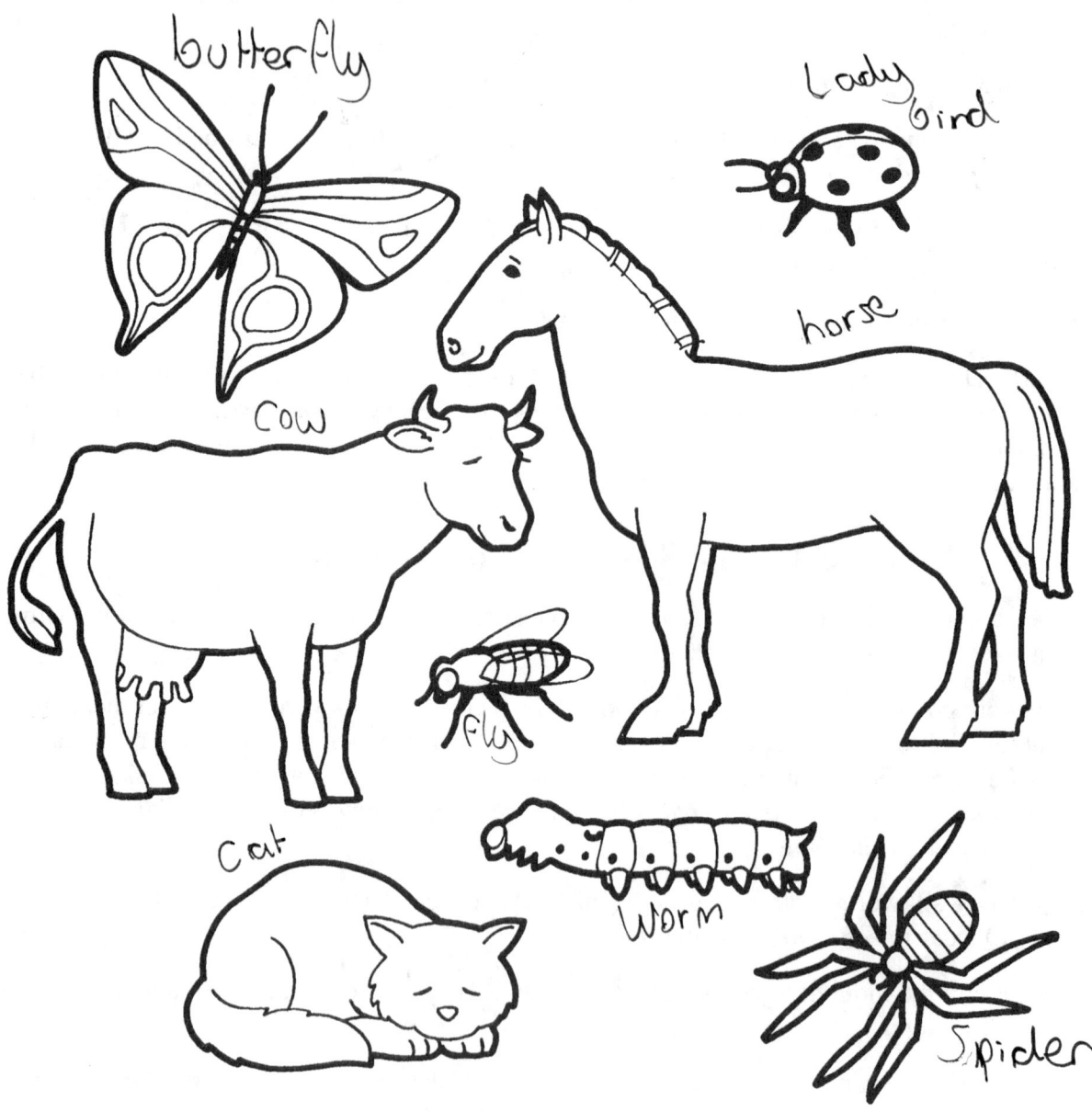

#2371 Thematic Unit—Silkworms and Mealworms © Teacher Created Materials, Inc.

Silkworms

Metamorphosis Cycle

Cut out the pictures of the metamorphosis of the silkworm to the silkworm moth. Paste them in the correct order on the page.

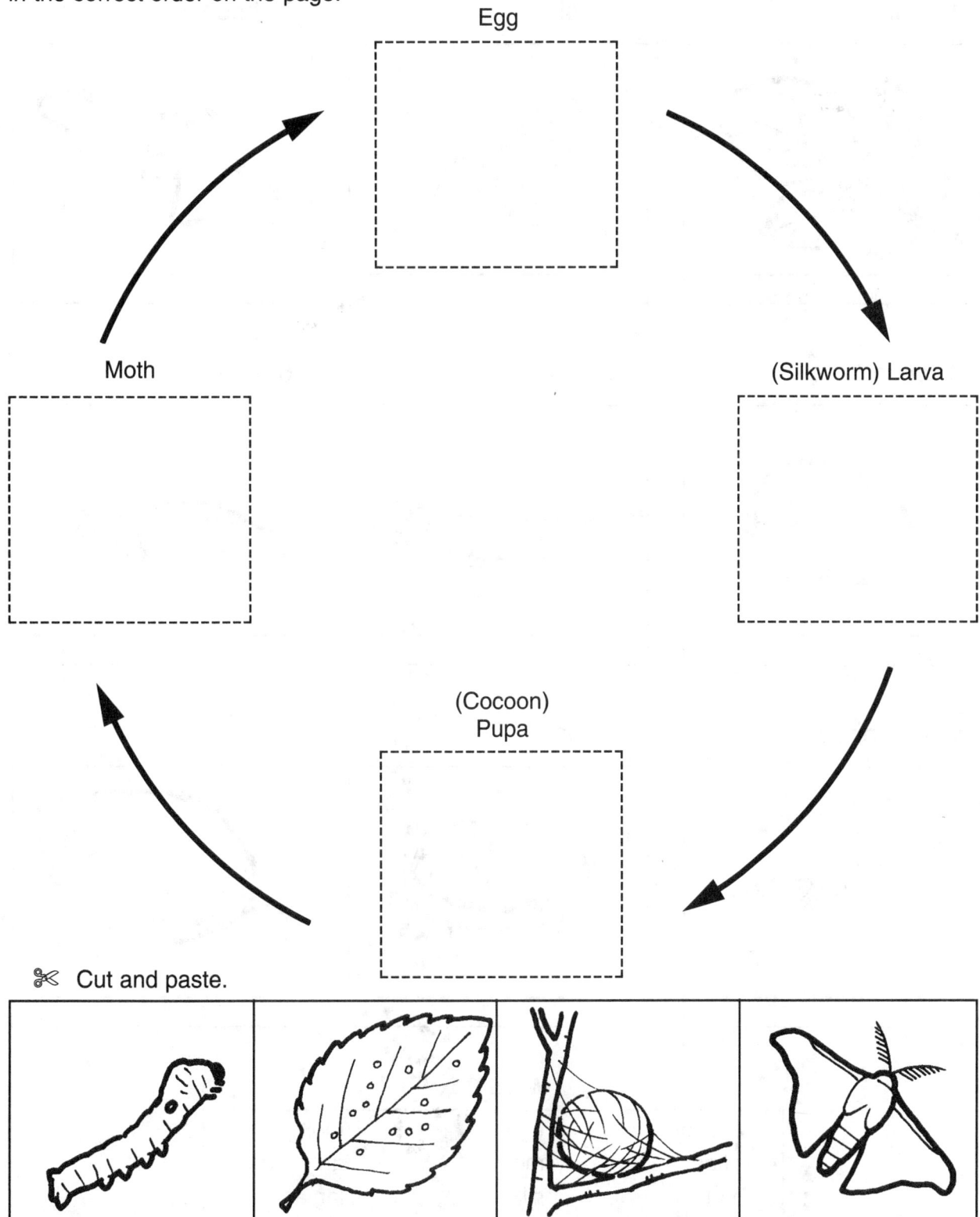

✂ Cut and paste.

Silkworms

Unscramble the Words

Unscramble the words that go with each picture. Use the word box to help you.

1. ealf

2. lksi
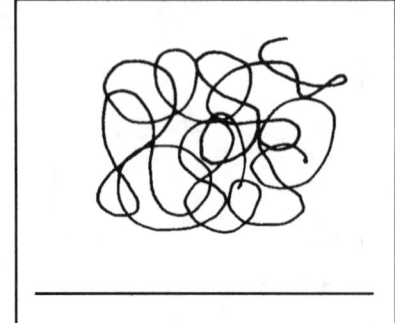

3. tmoh
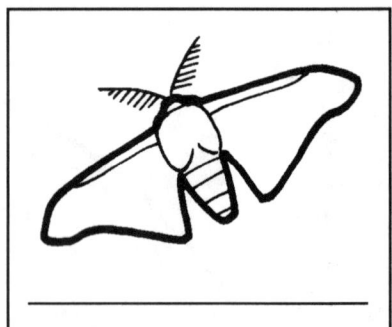

4. ooccon
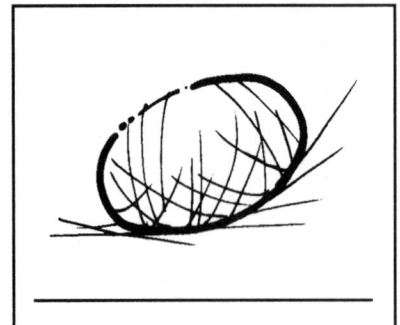

5. arvla
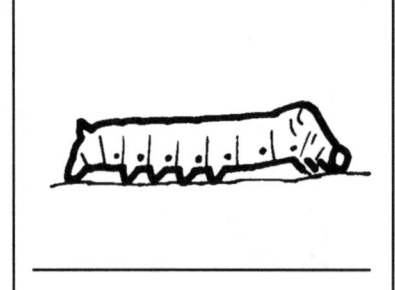

6. oltm
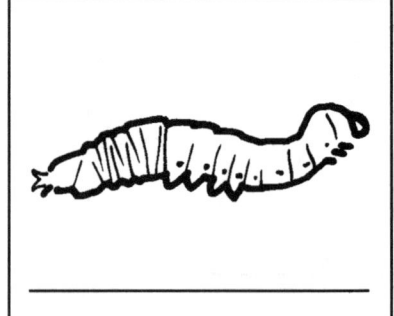

7. eantnnae

8. upap
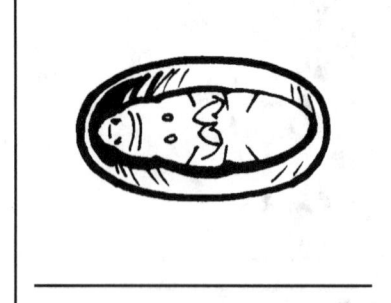

9. geg
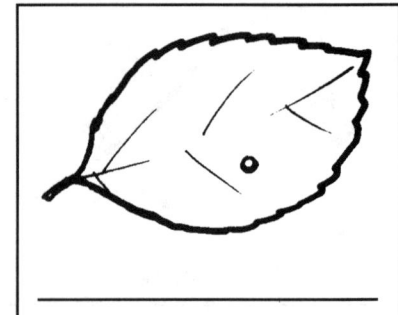

Word Box

cocoon	egg	molt
pupa	moth	antennae
leaf	silk	larva

Silkworms

Through the Eyes of a Silkworm

A silkworm has twelve simple eyes, but these eyes can only tell the difference between light and dark.

Set your classroom up into three center areas with props as described below. Explain to the children that they will pretend to be certain animals and find out how these animals see. Hold up a picture of a snake while explaining that a snake cannot blink or close its eyes. Ask everyone to "be a snake" and look around without blinking. It is not easy. Show children each center's animal by holding up a picture and demonstrating how to use that animal's seeing prop.

Silkworm (Discerns Darkness and Light)

- blindfolds (one per child)
- room that can be easily darkened

1. Place a blindfold on each child. Make sure they can't see!
2. Instruct the children to raise one hand when they think the lights are turned off and put hands down when lights are turned on.

Bee (Ultra-violet Colors)

- 8.5" x 11" (21.5 cm x 27.5 cm) sheet blue overhead transparency film
- empty eyeglass frames (one per child)
- pencils
- scissors
- cellophane tape

1. Place glasses (empty lens area) face down on blue film.
2. Trace outer edges of glasses with pencil; remove glasses and cut out.
3. Place blue "lenses" in front of glass lens frame; tape into place.

To use: Put eyeglasses on and look through.

Chameleon (Independent Eyes)

- two empty paper towel tubes with slightly bent ends (two per child)

To use: Hold one end of one paper towel tube up to left eye and angle other end upward. Simultaneously hold second paper towel tube up to right eye and angle downward.

© Teacher Created Materials, Inc.

The Empress and the Silkworm

by Lily Toy Hing

Summary

The Empress and the Silkworm is a beautifully illustrated picture book written about the Empress, Si Ling-Chi of China, during 2697 to 2597 B.C. Si Ling-Chi finds a silkworm cocoon in her hot tea that begins to unravel. Si Ling-Chi is intrigued with the silk strand. She begins winding the strand, which is almost a mile long! She discovers that this shining strand can be woven into the most beautiful fabric. But how can she convince her husband, the mighty Emperor, that this work should be done? This historically-based story shows the process of how a strand of silk from a cocoon is woven into beautiful silk fabric.

Sample Plan

Lesson 1
- Set up the Soft as Silk Bulletin Board (page 72) and the Silk or Not Silk Learning Center (page 74).
- Review Silkworm Instructions (page 9).
- Introduce *The Empress and the Silkworm* to your children and read the story.
- Complete the Story Sequence activity (page 20).
- Complete a daily journal question (page 45).

Lesson 2
- Read *The Empress and the Silkworm* to class again.
- Complete a daily journal question (page 45).
- Discover how silk is made (page 21).
- Use knowledge of silkworms via poetry ideas (page 48).
- Discuss that some creepy crawlies are helpful, while others are harmful (page 59).

Lesson 3
- Complete Compounded Animals on page 22.
- Complete a daily journal question (page 45).
- Complete the creative writing activity (page 19, #3).
- Practice place value (page 51).
- Review *The Empress and the Silkworm* and draw a favorite scene (page 60).
- Learn silkworm songs on pages 64 and 65.

Lesson 4
- Complete a daily journal question (page 45).
- Complete Silkworm Sentences (page 23).
- Research the strength of silk (page 56).
- Learn where silk is produced in the world today (page 58).
- Use popsicle puppets to enrich children's writing and story telling (page 63).
- Culminate with Show What You Know (page 68).

The Empress and the Silkworm

Overview of Activities

Setting the Stage

1. Assemble the Soft as Silk Bulletin Board (page 72) and the Silk or Not Silk Learning Center (page 74). If you have not done so yet, prepare the classroom door for the Classroom Door Activities on page 75.

2. Bring in pieces of silk clothing (i.e. ties, shirts, blouses, etc.). Allow children to feel these items and ask how the clothes were made.

3. Introduce Silky, the Silkworm (page 76). Discuss as a class behaviors that would get stickers put on the silkworm. Decide classroom rewards as a class as well. Be sure to award stickers daily so that it does not lose its effectiveness.

4. Review teacher information about the silkworm instructions and vocabulary on silkworms (pages 9, 69 and 70).

Enjoying the Book

1. Gather all of the children in a semi-circle on the floor, so that all can see the book. Look at the title. Who wrote the book? Who drew the pictures? Point out how colorful the pictures are. What might the story be about? Let many children make a prediction. Review with children what a silkworm is. Read aloud *The Empress and the Silkworm*, by Lily Toy Hong.

2. To help review the events of the story and to check the comprehension of your children, do the Story Sequence activity (page 20).

3. To promote confidence in reading, reread the story, but this time cover up certain words with self-sticking notes. Play a guessing game to figure out what the hidden words are.

4. Make an enlargement of the silkworm on page 78. This will be the center of a mobile. To reinforce high frequency words from the story, have children write out designated words for the silkworm to hold. Each time a story is read add new words. If possible, hang the mobile over the table where your silkworm books are displayed.

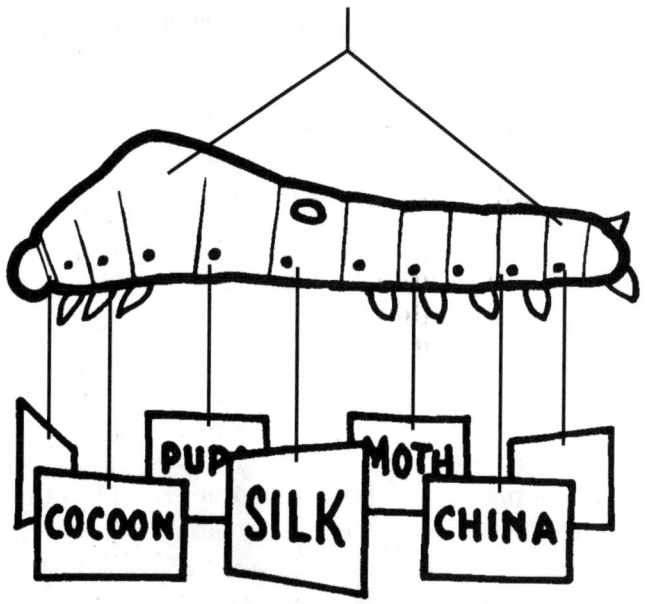

© Teacher Created Materials, Inc.

The Empress and the Silkworm

Overview of Activities (cont.)

Enjoying the Book (cont.)

5. To teach story elements, make an enlarged silkworm (page 78) on tagboard and laminate. Discuss the components of the story such as author, title, illustrator, setting, characters, goal, problem, ending, etc. Write a different component on each segment of the silkworm. Each day you may add information to the silkworm's segments about books or stories you have read.

6. Use the picture story of How Silk is Made (page 21) to reinforce concepts taught in the story *The Empress and the Silkworm*. Have the children read individually and then with a buddy.

7. Silkworm is a compound word. Teach the children about other compound words (page 22).

8. Enrich the knowledge your children have gained on the silkworm by writing poetry (page 48). Poetry allows one to express ideas and feelings not easily expressed in daily writing.

9. As a classroom, take a cocoon and unravel it. Measure how long the strand of silk is. How long did it take to unravel? Let the children make predictions of both. Refer back to the story to reread the length mentioned there.

10. Complete the Silkworm Sentences activity on page 23.

11. Reproduce page 60 and have the children draw a scene of their choice from the story, *The Empress and the Silkworm*. Play oriental music in the background while this activity is being completed. Allow the children to share their drawings with the class or with a partner; then display.

12. Gather the children together to learn the silkworm songs on pages 64 and 65. You may want to have a song contest and see if your children can create new words to a familiar tune about silkworms. Share the new songs with a neighboring class, recording the children as they are singing.

The Empress and the Silkworm

Overview of Activities *(cont.)*

Extending the Book

1. Have you ever kept a secret? Explain to the children that the secret of silk (its ability to be transformed into clothing) was kept for many, many years. Discuss how hard it would have been not to share that amazing discovery. Play the Telephone Game to see who can tell a secret the most accurately. The game is played when the first child whispers a secret into the second child's ear. This pattern continues until the secret has been shared through all the ears in the classroom. The last child that was whispered to then states what the original secret was. The secret will most certainly have changed!

2. Teach the children that some insects are helpful like the silkworm and some are harmful. Complete the Some Creepy Crawlies Help Us activity (page 59).

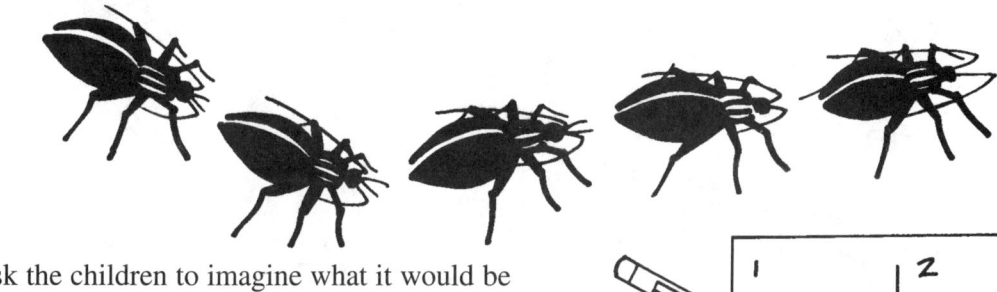

3. Ask the children to imagine what it would be like to be a silkworm. What would they do during the day? To start A Day in the Life of a Silkworm (page 49), give children about four minutes to begin working on this story idea. Then have them put their pencils down and pass their pages to a neighbor. The children then continue the story that is now in front of them. It's fun to see how the story ends up! (You can pass the stories a few more times.) Dramatize these stories using the popsicle puppets (page 63) or have them create some puppets of their own.

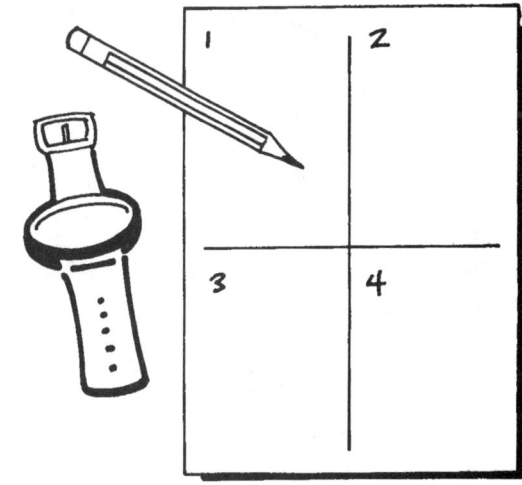

4. Research the strength of silk with How Strong is Silk (page 56). If possible, invite a guest speaker from a panty hose company (page 80) to come and talk to your classroom about the changes in the making of panty hose over time.

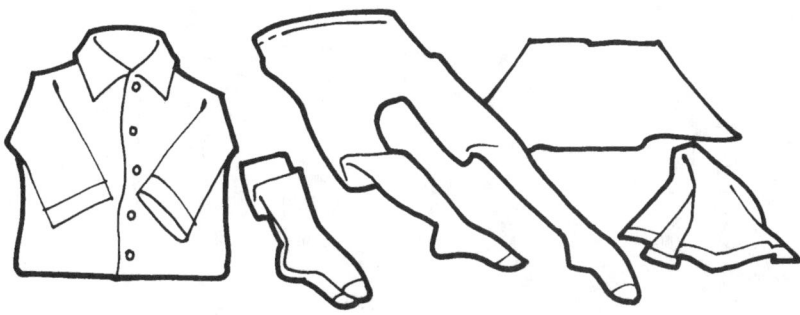

© Teacher Created Materials, Inc.   19   #2371 Thematic Unit—Silkworms and Mealworms

The Empress and the Silkworm

Story Sequence

Cut the pictures from the story *The Empress and the Silkworm* and paste them in correct order on a separate piece of paper or blank sentence strip. Label your pasted pictures in order 1, 2, 3, 4, 5, and 6.

#2371 Thematic Unit—Silkworms and Mealworms

How Silk is Made

The 🐛 silkworm spins 🥚 a cocoon. The 🥚 cocoon is made of 〰️ silk. These 🥚 🥚 cocoons are boiled in water. This gets the sticky substance off of the 🥚 🥚 cocoons. The workers then pick up the 〰️ silk 🧵 thread and start to spin it off the 🥚 cocoon. This 🧵 thread of 〰️ silk is put with other 🧵🧵 threads of 〰️ silk to make the strands thicker. The 🧵🧵 threads are spun many times. This makes the 〰️ silk softer. Workers then weave the 〰️ silk strands together to make 〰️ silk fabric. With 〰️ silk fabric, 〰️ silk 👕👕 shirts, 🎀🎀 scarves, and 👗👗 dresses are made. Do you have anything made of 〰️ silk?

The Empress and the Silkworm

Compounded Animals

Two words put together make a new word called a compound word.

Write the compound word for each animal.	Draw a picture of each compound word.

silk + worm = _____

gold + fish = _____

lady + bug = _____

butter + fly = _____

meal + worm = _____

blue + bird = _____

#2371 Thematic Unit—Silkworms and Mealworms   © Teacher Created Materials, Inc.

The Empress and the Silkworm

Silkworm Sentences

Connect the dots.

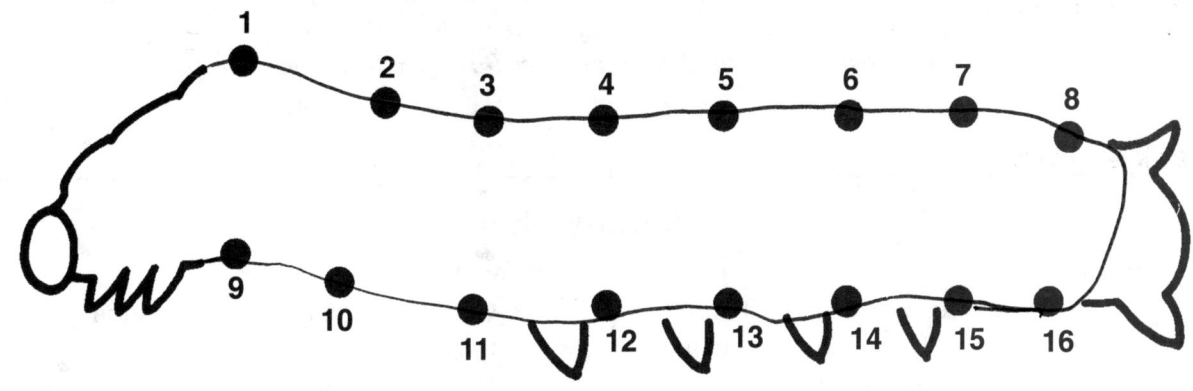

Cut out the three sentences that are true about a silkworm.
Paste the sentences in the boxes above.

Silkworms like to eat Mulberry leaves.

A silkworm is really a worm.

Silkworms are the larva of a moth.

A silkworm spins its cocoon out of silk.

A silkworm turns into a butterfly.

My Mealworm Book

(A Make-It-Yourself Book)

Summary

These easy-to-make booklets provide your children with basic mealworm knowledge. **My Mealworm Book** *pages are accompanied by hands-on science experiments that will enrich your study of mealworms. Instructions for assembling the* **My Mealworm Book** *are found on page 30.*

Sample Plan

Lesson 1

- Set up the Mealworm Mania T-shirt bulletin board (page 73) and classroom door learning centers (page 75).
- Review Mealworm Instructions (page 28).
- Complete the KWL activity as a class (page 25, #7).
- Construct Mealworm Habitats (page 69).
- Discuss Silkworm and Mealworm Vocabulary words (page 70).
- Complete a daily journal question (page 45).
- Construct *My Mealworm Book* (page 30), one per child.
- Look through *My Mealworm Book*.
- Complete Look at the Mealworm! (page 34) and pages 1 and 2 of *My Mealworm Book* (page 29).

Lesson 2

- Learn the parts of the Tenebrio beetle (page 53) and complete page 3 of *My Mealworm Book* (page 29).
- Learn how mealworms walk and find bran (page 37); complete page 4 of *My Mealworm Book* (page 29).
- Complete Create-a-Sentence (page 47).
- Sing Mealworm Songs and Finger Play (pages 64 and 65).

Lesson 3

- Complete a daily journal question (page 45).
- Reread first four pages of *My Mealworm Book*. Find out what mealworms will eat (page 38).
- Begin to experiment to find out how the amount of food affects mealworm populations (page 39).
- Complete the Mealworm Maze activity (page 40).
- Observe how many segments a mealworm has compared to your index finder with a magnifying glass. Complete page 5 of *My Mealworm Book* (page 30).

Lesson 4

- Discover which colors mealworms prefer (page 41) and complete page 6 of *My Mealworm Book* (page 30).
- Make mealworm life cycle books (page 43).
- Make the Creepy Crawly Mealworm art project (page 62).
- Cook recipes made with mealworms in mind (page 66). These recipes can also be sent home to be made as a family.
- Complete culminating game activities (page 67).

Mealworms

Overview of Activities

Setting the Stage

1. Assemble the Mealworm T-Shirt Mania bulletin board. T-shirts are a way for people to express themselves. Have the children design a T-shirt on what they think about mealworms. (For example: Mealworms are wiggly! Mealworms are fast! Mealworms tickle my hand! Mealworms are fun!) Have the children do their design in pencil on the T-shirt pattern (page 73) and then color the T-shirt. To display in your classroom, hang a clothesline across the room and hang up the T-shirts with clothespins. As an extension, have the children bring in actual white T-shirts and make designs on them using fabric paints. Wear these T-shirts during the unit, or as a part of the last day's culminating activities.

2. Prepare the door with Door Invitations (page 75).

3. Copy the second Parent Letter (page 71) and have it ready to send home on the appropriate day.

4. Continue with the daily journal entry topics (page 45).

5. Carefully read and review the mealworm instructions on page 28, the safety rules on page 69, and the mealworm vocabulary words on page 70.

6. Have the children construct their mealworm habitats (page 69).

7. Gather the children around to look at a mealworm. Discuss the differences and similarities with the silkworm. On a large piece of butcher paper create a KWL chart. Follow the directions outlined on page 6, #6, this time focusing on mealworms rather than silkworms.

8. Introduce the behavioral incentive Dot-to-Dot Mealworm (page 76). Discuss with your children possible rewards.

© Teacher Created Materials, Inc. 25 #2371 Thematic Unit—Silkworms and Mealworms

Mealworms

Overview of Activities *(cont.)*

Enjoying the Book

1. Follow the assembling directions (page 30) to make the *My Mealworm Book.* You will want to have these books made ahead of time for the children. Each page has a different fact and corresponding hands-on science experiment or activity.

2. After reading *My Mealworm Book* as a class, compare mealworms and silkworms. How are they alike? How are they different? Make a Venn diagram class chart for the children to add information to throughout this unit of study.

3. Children will be using scientific skills in the How Do Mealworms Find Bran experiment? (page 37). As an extension to this lesson, ask the children to talk about how they get food for themselves. Is there a pattern to their eating? How do they get their food?

4. Review with the children how to construct a complete simple sentence (must have a subject/noun and a verb). When you feel your the children are ready, complete the Create-a-Sentence activity on page 47.

5. Enrich addition skills with Mealworm Mania (page 52). Be sure that you have explained how to use the code on this page to insure proper use.

6. The Tenebrio beetle is the adult mealworm. Children will learn the parts of a beetle with Beetle Mania (page 53). As an extension, get a book on beetles (Bibliography, page 80) and look at the varieties of beetles. Invite an entomologist or someone who collects bugs as a hobby to come to your classroom.

7. Send home the second parent letter (page 71). Discuss with the children the types of food they think that the mealworm might eat. Ask them to bring in tiny bits of samples to try to get the mealworms to eat. Begin the activity What Do Mealworms Eat? (page 38) the next morning.

8. Children will enjoy designing a maze for mealworms to pass through (page 40). Place a spoonful of bran at the end of the maze (incentive for the mealworm). Remember to choose active mealworms and don't make the maze too long or children will lose interest.

Overview of Activities *(cont.)*

Enjoying the Book *(cont.)*

9. Ask the children what their favorite colors are. Why do they like those colors? Mealworms prefer certain colors, too. See if your children can hypothesize and discover why mealworms like certain colors using the experiment on page 41.

10. To review the life cycle of a mealworm, construct life cycle mealworm books (page 43).

Extending the Book

1. Make plans to do some cooking in the classroom. Mealworms like to eat many of the same things humans do. Mealworms are often found eating stored grains and bran. Sample some bran. Then prepare the bran and cornmeal recipes found on page 66.

2. The Creepy Crawly Mealworm art project (page 62) is fun and easy to make. Be sure to begin saving toilet-tissue rolls ahead of time to ensure that all the children have plenty.

3. Bring music and rhythm into your classroom with the activities on pages 64 and 65. Encourage the children to make up their own verses or songs about a mealworm and Tenebrio beetle. Act like mealworms or beetles as you sing the newly created verses.

4. Complete the culminating activities (page 67). Create a mealworm and silkworm presentation to share with another class in your school. Brainstorm activities the children can develop and share based on what they have learned throughout the entire unit. Be sure to include all the children in the presentation.

5. Review the KWL charts (page 6, #6). Spend time discussing what they have learned. Ask the children to write their thoughts in their journals.

6. When you have completed this unit, present the awards on page 77. Hand out pencil toppers (page 76) to commemorate completing the unit, or present the toppers throughout the unit as incentives.

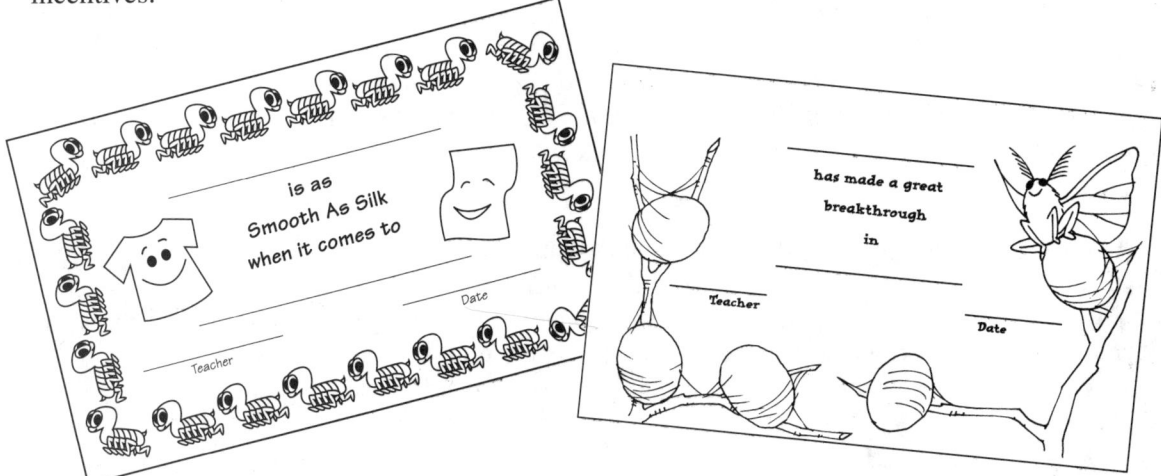

Mealworms

Mealworm Instructions

This page will give you the information you will need to know in order to successfully raise mealworms in your classroom. Please read instructions carefully.

What are Mealworms?

Mealworms are not really worms. They are the larvae of the Tenebrio beetle. They are actually caterpillars. Mealworms are considered scavengers and are among the largest insects that infest stored products. They prefer to feed on decaying grain or milled cereals in damp, poor condition. They are usually found in places not frequently disturbed, such as dark corners. Indoors they are usually found infesting cornmeal, flour, cake mixes, and cereals.

Identification

Mealworms have a smooth, shiny, highly polished, hard, worm-like, segmented body. They are about $1/8$ inch (.3 cm) thick and up to $1\text{-}1/4$ inches (3.14 cm) long at maturity. Young mealworms are white or yellow, and will darken with age. Mealworms are the young larvae of the Tenebrio beetle. The Tenebrio beetles are robust, hard-shelled, black, and nearly $3/4$ inch (1.89 cm) long, resembling many ground beetles in size, shape and color.

Life Cycle

Each female Tenebrio beetle lays about 275 eggs. Times required for each stage of the beetle under average conditions are: 4 weeks for the egg, 10 weeks for the larva, 3 weeks for the pupa, and 4 weeks for the beetle.

Culturing Mealworms

To culture mealworms, use a plastic, metal, or glass container with smooth sides to prevent escape. (Recycled margarine or butter containers work well.) A wide-mouth gallon jar can easily hold 1,000 mealworms!

Place an equal amount of bran and mealworms in the chosen container. Mealworms and bran can be purchased at most pet stores. Occasionally lay slices of apple, potato, or over-ripe banana in with the mealworms for moisture.

> *Mealworms thrive in a warm 80-90 degrees F (27 degrees C) environment. To maintain the larvae in a state of dormancy, cover the container with a lid and set in a refrigerator at 40-50 degrees F (5 degrees C). Mealworms will die at lower temperatures!*

Keep the mealworms in the refrigerator and each day pull them out about 15 minutes before you plan to do experiments. After you have finished all of the experiments using the mealworms, have each child place some mealworms in their prepared mealworm habitat (page 69). Do not place containers back in refrigerator. The mealworms will now begin their life cycle within a few days.

Mealworms

My Mealworm Book Overview

Teacher Note: Before following these page-by-page usage directions, make as many copies as needed (one book per child) of the *My Mealworm Book* following the assembling directions on page 30.

Page 1: A mealworm looks like a worm, but it is not really a worm.

1. Have children color the mealworm with a white or cream-colored crayon.

2. Complete the experiment Look at the Mealworm! (page 34).

Page 2: A mealworm has three pairs of legs in front and four pairs of legs in back. A mealworm has one leg that does not move on the end of its body.

1. Have children color the mealworm and then fill in where the legs go on their mealworm by showing them a picture of a mealworm (clip art, page 78).

2. Complete the experiment, How Do Mealworms Walk? (page 36).

3. Have a group of children demonstrate how a mealworm walk. Children should use their arms to resemble the legs of the mealworm. Remember you will need thirteen segments for one mealworm.

Page 3: A mealworm is the larva of a Tenebrio beetle. A Tenebrio beetle is black and has a hard shell.

1. Review with the children the meaning of the word metamorphosis to help in studying the life cycle of a mealworm.

2. Have children color each stage of the life cycle. Be sure the beetle is colored black. Also have the children trace the stage numerals 1 through 4.

3. Complete the Magnificent Mealworms activity (page 43).

Page 4: What does a mealworm eat? A mealworm likes to eat stored grains and dry oatmeal.

1. Complete the experiments, How Do Mealworms Find Bran? (page 37) and What Do Mealworms Eat? (page 38).

2. Have children draw or cut out pictures from magazines things a mealworm likes to eat (cereals, grains, rice, corn, pancake mix, etc.).

3. Set up and begin the class experiment, Mealworms and Apples (page 39).

© Teacher Created Materials, Inc.

Mealworms

My Mealworm Book Overview *(cont.)*

Page 5: A mealworm's body is divided into segments so that it can be flexible.

1. Discuss the meaning of the word segments (separated parts).
2. Have children wiggle their fingers. Talk about how the segments in their fingers make it easier for them to bend their fingers. This is also true for the mealworm's body.
3. Have the children trace the dashed lines (three for the index finger and 13 for the mealworm) and color the finger and mealworm on page 5 of *My Mealworm Book*.
4. Complete the experiment Mealworm Maze (page 40).

Page 6: Mealworms can be found in dark, damp places.

1. Have children complete the experiment, A Mealworm's Favorite Color (page 41).
2. Have children draw mealworms in the box in such a way as to represent where mealworms prefer to hide out (the shaded, darker side). (Optional: Glue down uncooked grains of white rice to symbolize the mealworms.)

My Mealworm Book Assembling Instructions

Supplies Needed To Make Books

- construction paper (9" x 12"/23 cm x 30 cm)
- reproduced copies of pages 1–6 (pages 31–33)
- scissors
- stapler
- felt tip marker

Instructions for Making One Book

1. Cut the construction paper in half so you have two pieces (6" x 9"; 15 cm x 23 cm). Lay one piece on a flat surface.
2. Stack the reproduced pages one (top) to six (bottom). Place stacked pages directly on top of construction paper (make certain the book page's left edges are flush with the construction paper's left edge).
3. Place the second half sheet of construction paper on top. Line up the left edges of all sheets; staple them along the edge to create a spine.
4. Using the felt tip marker on the construction paper cover, write *My Mealworm Book* and Name (see illustration at right).

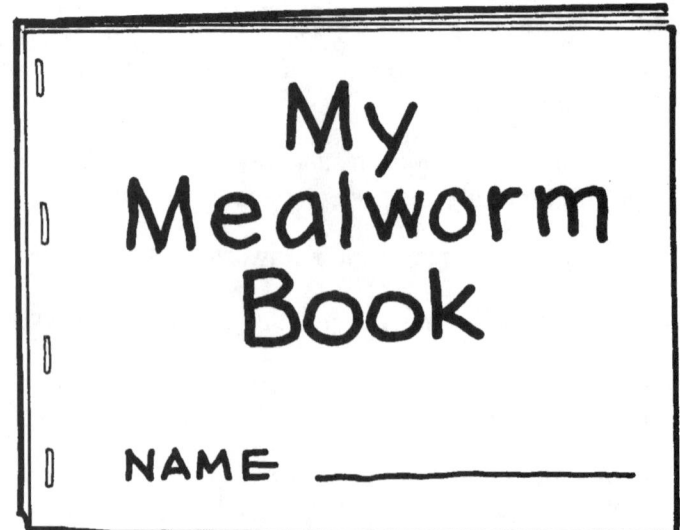

#2371 Thematic Unit—Silkworms and Mealworms

My Mealworm Book

A mealworm looks like a worm, but it is not really a worm.

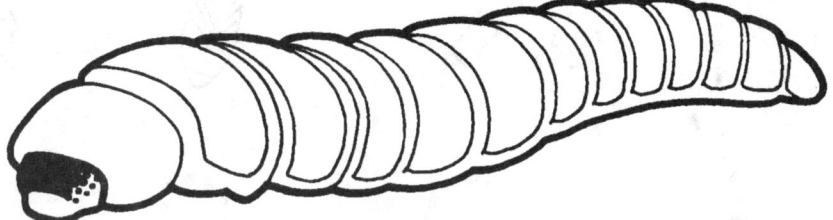

1

A mealworm has three pairs of legs in front and four pairs of legs in back.

A mealworm has one leg that does not move on the end of its body.

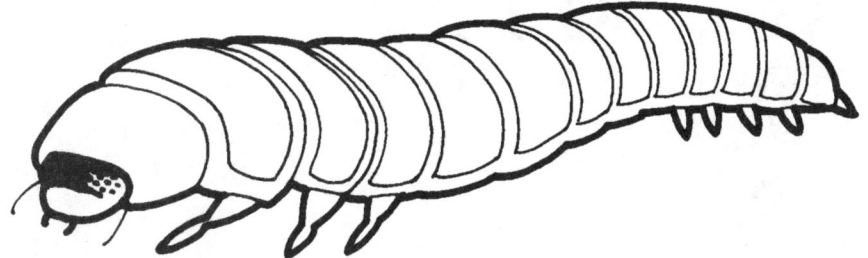

2

Mealworms

My Mealworm Book (cont.)

A mealworm is the larva of a Tenebrio beetle. A Tenebrio beetle is black and has a hard shell.

Stage 1 2 3 4

3

What does a mealworm eat? A mealworm likes to eat stored grains and dry oatmeal.

4

My Mealworm Book (cont.)

A mealworm's body is divided into segments so that it can be flexible.

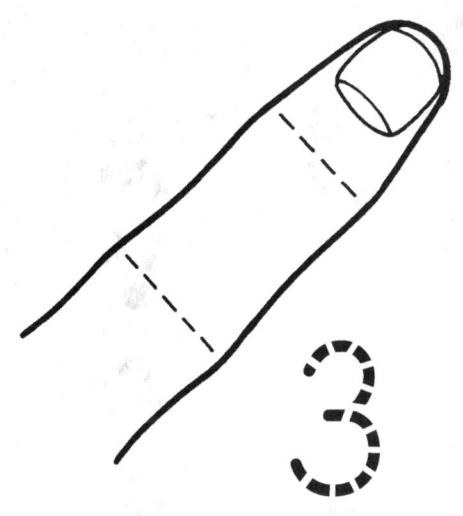
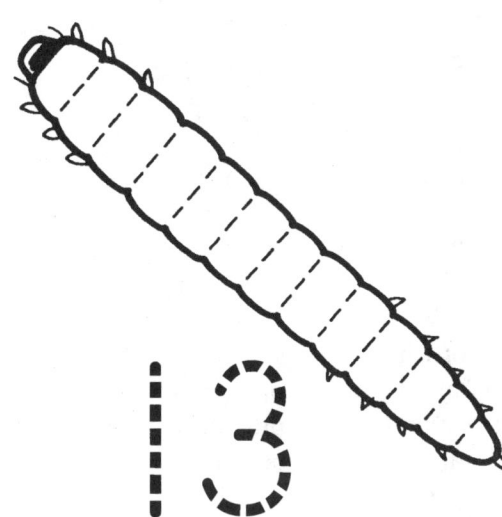

5

Mealworms can be found in dark, damp places.

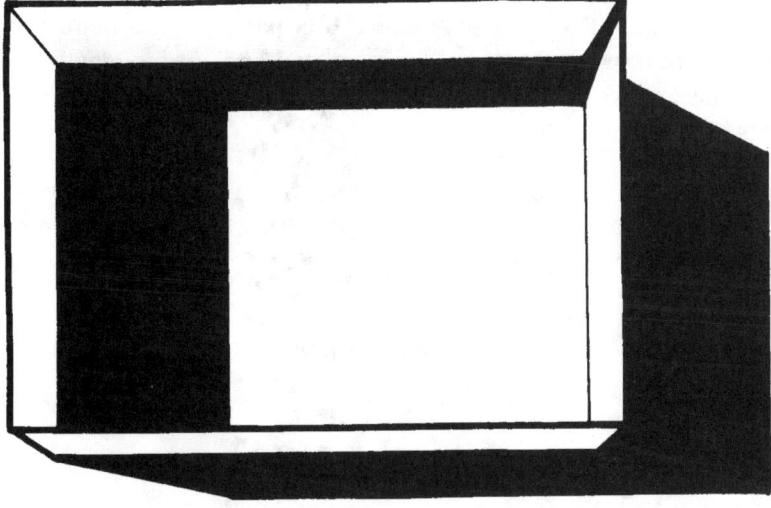

6

Mealworms

Look at the Mealworm!

Teacher Note: This page should be done only after reviewing the safety rules for handling mealworms (pages 28 and 69).

Materials

- mealworm for each child
- white piece of paper for each child
- pencil
- copies of page 35 for each child
- magnifying glass for each child

Preparation

Place a piece of white paper on the desk of each child. *Children need to watch their mealworms at all times.* Sometimes the mealworms will wander off and it can be hard to find them. They might even fall off the table or desk. Keeping them on a piece of paper makes it easier to keep track of them. (Note: Do not throw these papers away. They can be reused for each experiment.)

Since mealworms cannot talk and answer questions, remind the children that it will be necessary to watch them very closely in order to learn more about them. Discuss with the children the concept of how we get to know a new person. What types of things do we do? Ask questions, talk to them, observe them, etc. They will need to do the same with their mealworms, except expect to be answered!

Directions

1. Distribute a mealworm to each child to observe. Ask them to name their mealworms.

2. Distribute the magnifying glasses; observe mealworms closely. Point out that a mealworm has three pairs of legs in front, with claw-like feet, and four pairs toward the rear with suction-cup feet. A leg that does not move is located at the very "tail end" of the mealworm. A mealworm has two short antennae. Its eyes are not visible. The mealworm's body is divided into thirteen segments in order to be flexible.

3. Ask the children if they can somehow make their mealworms respond to their presence. Ask each child to gently blow on his or her mealworm; call the mealworm by its given name; touch the mealworm with one finger; put a pencil near the mealworm, but not directly touching the mealworm; etc. What made the mealworm respond?

4. The children then record the things they tried to do with their mealworms (page 35), as well as draw an illustration of their magnified mealworms.

Look at the Mealworm *(cont.)*

See page 34 for suggested use.

In the magnifying glass, draw an illustration of your mealworm.

Things I tried:	What the mealworm did:
Called the mealworm by name	
Put a pencil near it	
Blew gently on the mealworm	
Touched it gently with my finger	

Mealworms

How Do Mealworms Walk?

Materials

- white sheet of paper per child (observation area)
- one mealworm per child
- one copy of the Mealworm Questions (below) per child*

Directions

1. Gather children around to watch a container of mealworms. Let the children observe and share their observations aloud. What are the mealworms doing? What do you see? What do you hear? What do all these mealworms remind you of?

2. Provide each child with one mealworm on his or her observation area white sheet. After observing the mealworms for a few moments, hand out the Mealworm Questions; allow time for children to answer the questions by observing their mealworms.

* Instead of providing questions to each child, you may want to copy the questions onto the chalkboard or chart paper. Work through these questions one at a time, discussing each as a class. Record answers/responses on the chalkboard, chart paper, or have the children record responses on their own copies of questions.

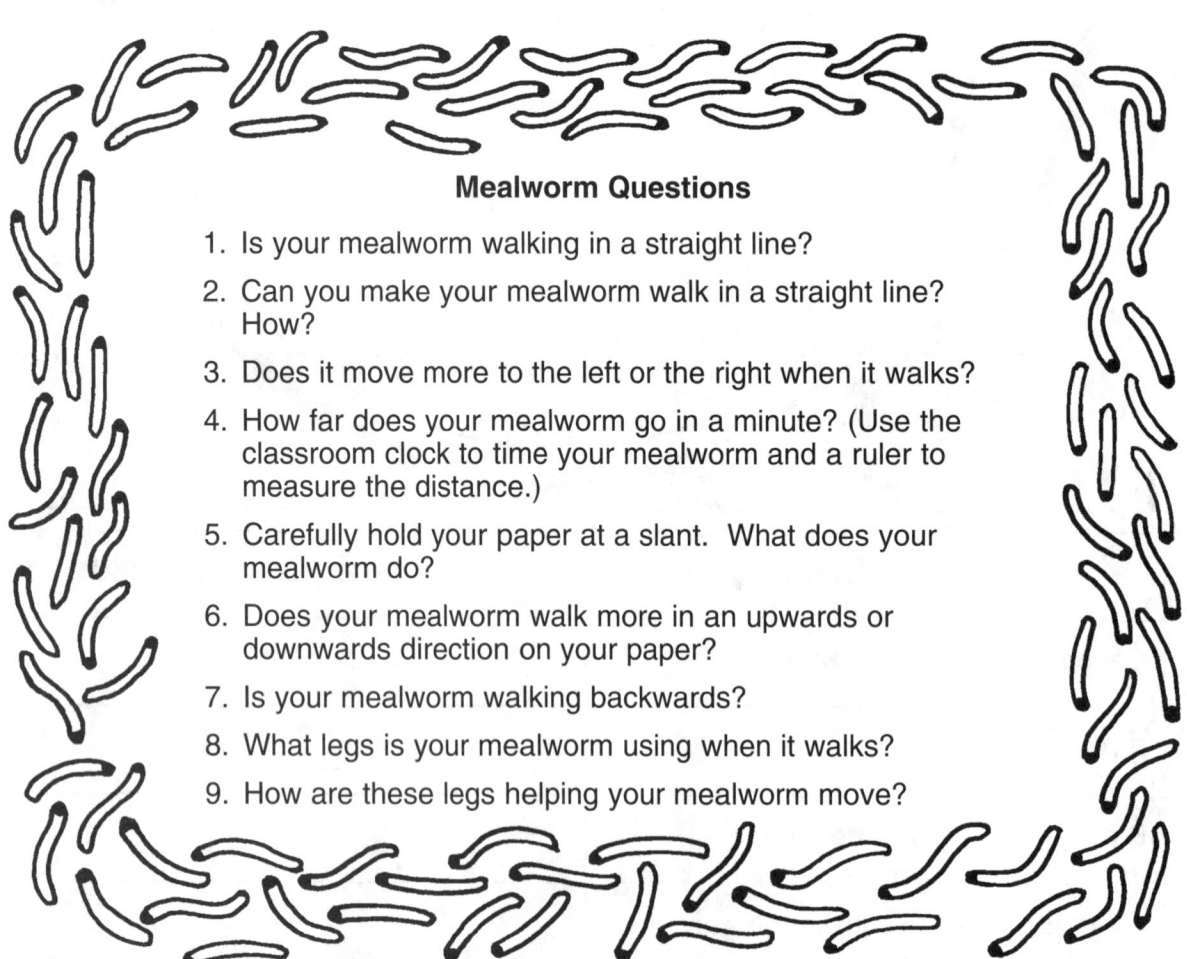

Mealworm Questions

1. Is your mealworm walking in a straight line?
2. Can you make your mealworm walk in a straight line? How?
3. Does it move more to the left or the right when it walks?
4. How far does your mealworm go in a minute? (Use the classroom clock to time your mealworm and a ruler to measure the distance.)
5. Carefully hold your paper at a slant. What does your mealworm do?
6. Does your mealworm walk more in an upwards or downwards direction on your paper?
7. Is your mealworm walking backwards?
8. What legs is your mealworm using when it walks?
9. How are these legs helping your mealworm move?

Mealworms

How Do Mealworms Find Bran?

Materials

- white sheet of paper per child (observation area)
- one mealworm per child
- approximately 1 tablespoon (15 mL) of bran per child
- pencil
- three different colored crayons per child

Directions

1. Explain to the children that the purpose of the experiment today is to see how a mealworm goes about finding bran. Have each child make a hypothesis as to how a mealworm might find bran. (i.e. the mealworm wanders back and forth; the mealworm walks straight to the bran; the mealworm walks quickly/slowly to the bran, etc.).

2. In the observation area (white sheet of paper), place a small pile of bran near the left edge. Have each child place his or her mealworm on the right side of paper, also near the edge.

3. Ask the children to closely observe has the mealworm works its way towards the bran. (Ask the children not to blow, push or touch the mealworm.)

4. Using a crayon, have the children trace the path the mealworm took get to the bran.

5. Have the children repeat the experiment steps 2 and 3 two more times, each time using a different mealworm. After each mealworm treks across the paper, have the children use a different color crayon to make the mealworm's pathway on a white sheet of paper. Place the mealworms back in their habitat.

6. To conclude, meet together as a class. Display and discuss the findings of each child's mealworm traveling paths. Then have children share their conclusions on how a mealworm gets to the bran.

7. Have each child record their personal thoughts based on his or her white sheet of paper containing the mealworms, paths; display the path sheets with conclusion statements.

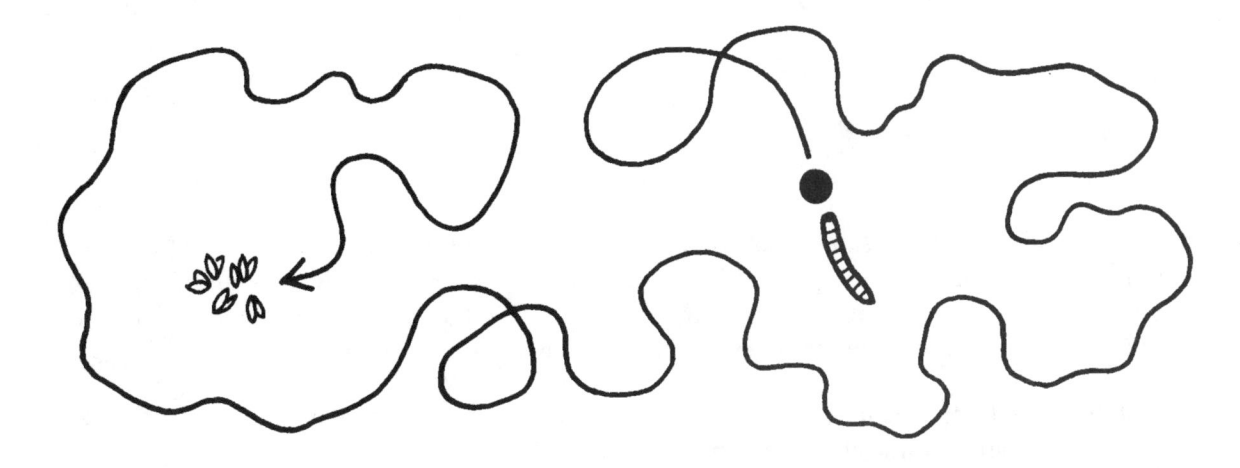

© Teacher Created Materials, Inc. #2371 Thematic Unit—Silkworms and Mealworms

Mealworms

What Do Mealworms Eat?

Teacher's Note: Begin this activity by asking the children the day before the experiment what they think mealworms might like to eat. Record observations on a chart or on the chalkboard. As a homework assignment (See the parent letter on page 71), have the children bring in small samples of food items they think a mealworm might like to eat.

Materials

- white sheet of paper per child (observation area)
- one mealworm per child
- samples of food (i.e. bits of lettuce, apple, cereal, potatoes, candy, sugar, salt, grains, pancake mix, etc.)

Directions

1. Lead a discussion on things we already know a mealworm will eat, such as bran and apple pieces.
2. Have each child place a mealworm on the white sheet of paper (observation area). Give bits of food to each child to give to the mealworm. What do the mealworms do? Verbalize or record after each food item how the mealworms reacted to each food item.

Mealworms like to eat . . .	Mealworms do not like to eat . . .

When finished testing all of the samples of food, have the children put away their white papers, mealworms, and food samples. Meet together as a whole class. Have the children share aloud with the class the things that the mealworms would eat and the things that the mealworms would not eat. Ask the children why or why not? Are the things the mealworms ate similar to bran or apple pieces?

Make a list of all the things the mealworms ate and a list of things that they would not eat. Record these on the chalkboard or on white butcher paper.

Mealworms

Mealworms and Apples

Mealworms are the larvae of the black Tenebrio beetles. Mealworms are sold in pet stores as live food for animals like snakes and lizards. We can also find them in bags and boxes of food like grain and cornmeal that have been left on the shelf too long.

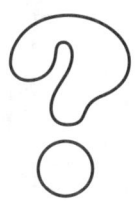

Will there be **more** or **less** mealworms if there is a lot of food for them to eat?

Mark the **more** or **less** box.

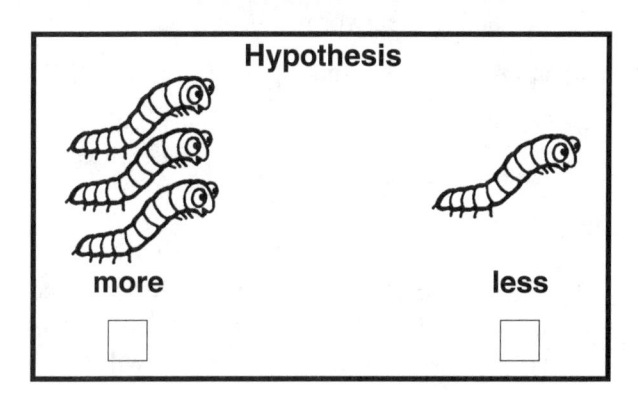

Hypothesis

more ☐   less ☐

Materials
- 20 mealworms
- raw bran
- apple slices
- 2 shoe boxes

Procedure

1. Put ½ inch (1.3 cm) thick layer of raw bran in the bottom of each shoe box; label one box Box A and the other box Box B.
2. Put one apple cut into four quarters in Box A.
3. Put only 1 piece (one quarter) of an apple in Box B.
4. Add 10 healthy mealworms to each box.
5. Each week for the next four weeks, add the same ratio of apples to Boxes A and B.
6. At the end of the fourth week, count the mealworms in each box. Record the numbers below.

Mealworm Box A	Mealworm Box B
I counted _____ mealworms.	I counted _____ mealworms.

My Conclusion

Circle **more** or **less** and complete sentence.

There were _____ mealworms in the box with _____ food
            (more/less)   (more/less)

because _____

_____.

© Teacher Created Materials, Inc.

Mealworms

Mealworm Maze

Materials (per pair of children)

- white sheet of paper (observation area)
- one active mealworm
- approximately 1 tablespoon (15 mL) of bran
- one wooden ruler and one clear plastic ruler
- Cuisenaire® rods and/or blocks

Directions

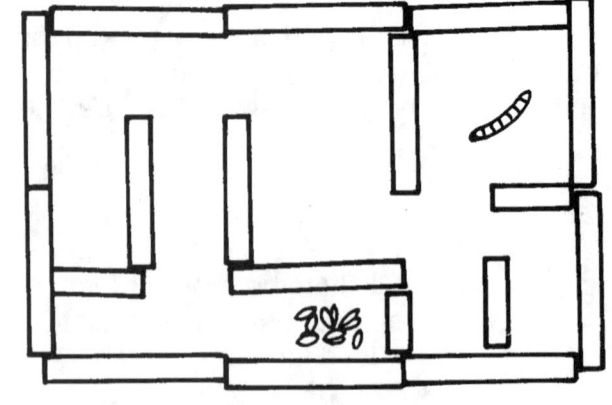

1. Have one child hold the wooden ruler perpendicular to the table (see diagram below) to form a tall wall. The other child then places the mealworm next to the base of the wooden ruler, observing to see if the mealworm will climb up and over the ruler or just move alongside of it.

2. Place the wooden ruler flat on the table to create a low wall. Place the mealworm next to it and see if it will walk up and over or move along the side the low wall.

3. Place one end of the wooden ruler off the edge of a desk or table to create an overhanging wall. Place the mealworm next to the part of the ruler that is still on the flat surface and see what happens when the mealworm moves towards the overhanging end of ruler. (Note: Have one child stand with hands cupped under the ruler to catch the mealworm if it falls off the ruler.)

4. Have the children repeat steps one through three with a clear plastic ruler next to the mealworm. Does the mealworm react differently with a see-through wall?

5. Now spend time discussing as a class what a maze is. Using the information gathered from steps one through four, have the children use Cuisenaire® rods and blocks; rulers and other materials to create a maze (don't make it too long or complex; the mealworm will lose interest). Put a spoonful of bran at the end of the maze. Place the mealworm at the beginning of the maze. See if the mealworm can make it through the maze and find the bran.

6. To conclude, have each team draw a "bird's-eye view" of the maze and the mealworm's path in tackling the maze to try to get to the bran. Display the drawings.

Mealworms

A Mealworm's Favorite Color

Materials (per pair of children)

- 5" (12 cm) square piece of red, blue, yellow, and black paper
- small circle (about the size of a half dollar) of white paper
- two active mealworms
- data chart (page 42)

Teacher Note: During this experiment, children will find out if mealworms prefer light colors over dark colors. Begin meeting as a whole group and asking the children to share what their favorite colors are. Discuss the concept of light and dark colors using color names they have mentioned.

Procedure

1. Distribute to each pair of children the four square and one circle pieces of paper. Ask the children to arrange the pieces as follows (You may want to draw a color diagram on chart paper and display it to help them with correct placement.):

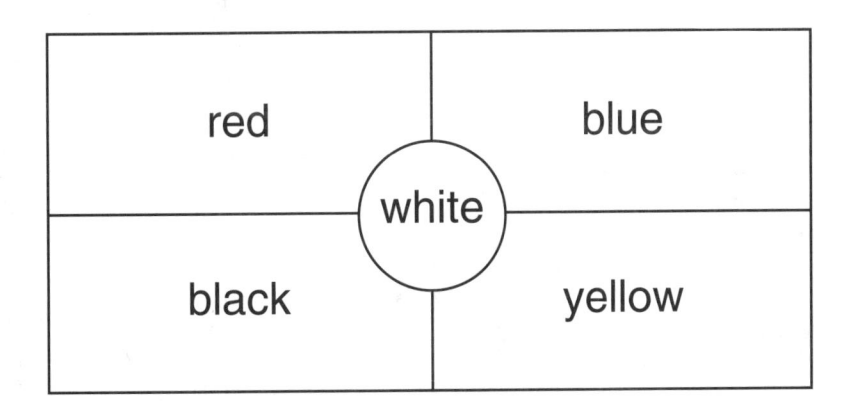

red	blue
black	yellow

(white circle in center)

2. Give each team two active mealworms. Ask one child to cradle the mealworms in one hand. Ask the team to observe their mealworms closely to determine a way in which to tell the two mealworms apart. Ask them to name their mealworms. Then ask them to record the two names on their data sheet.

3. Have the teams place their two mealworms on the white circle and observe closely what their mealworms do. The children are then to place a tally mark on the data sheet every time one of the mealworm moves into a certain colored square (be certain they know which mealworm is which). Have the children observe and tally for approximately four or five minutes.

4. Now meet together as a class to share and discuss each team's results. Write a class conclusion statement on chart paper; display tallied data sheets around the written conclusion.

5. If using *My Mealworm Book*, complete page 6 (see page 30).

© Teacher Created Materials, Inc.

Mealworms

Favorite Color Data Chart

Make a tally mark under the color to show where the mealworms traveled.

Name of Mealworm	Stayed on White	Visited Yellow	Visited Red	Visited Black	Visited Blue

We observed our mealworms for _____ minutes.

Magnificent Mealworms

Mealworms eat "meal," any grain that is easy to eat such as bran or corn, breakfast cereal, and dry dog food. Mealworms also need food with small amounts of water in it, like a slice of apple, carrot, or potato.

Mealworms begin as an egg. The egg will hatch larvae called mealworms. The mealworms begin to grow. They form into pupas, a cocoon-like stage. The pupa is like a teenager, between being a child (mealworm) and being an adult (beetle). Out of the pupa comes a Tenebrio beetle. Female beetles lay eggs. The eggs hatch into newborn baby mealworms and the life cycle starts all over again. Can you find all the stages of the life cycle in your container of mealworms?

Let's make a life cycle book about your mealworms.

Materials

- one 9" by 12" (23 cm x 30 cm) page of colored construction paper, cut in half lengthwise, then glued together at two ends to form one long strip (Allow strip to dry.)
- one copy of the Life Cycle of a Mealworm (page 44)

Directions

1. Fold the strip of construction paper into four equal sections, as shown in the picture below:

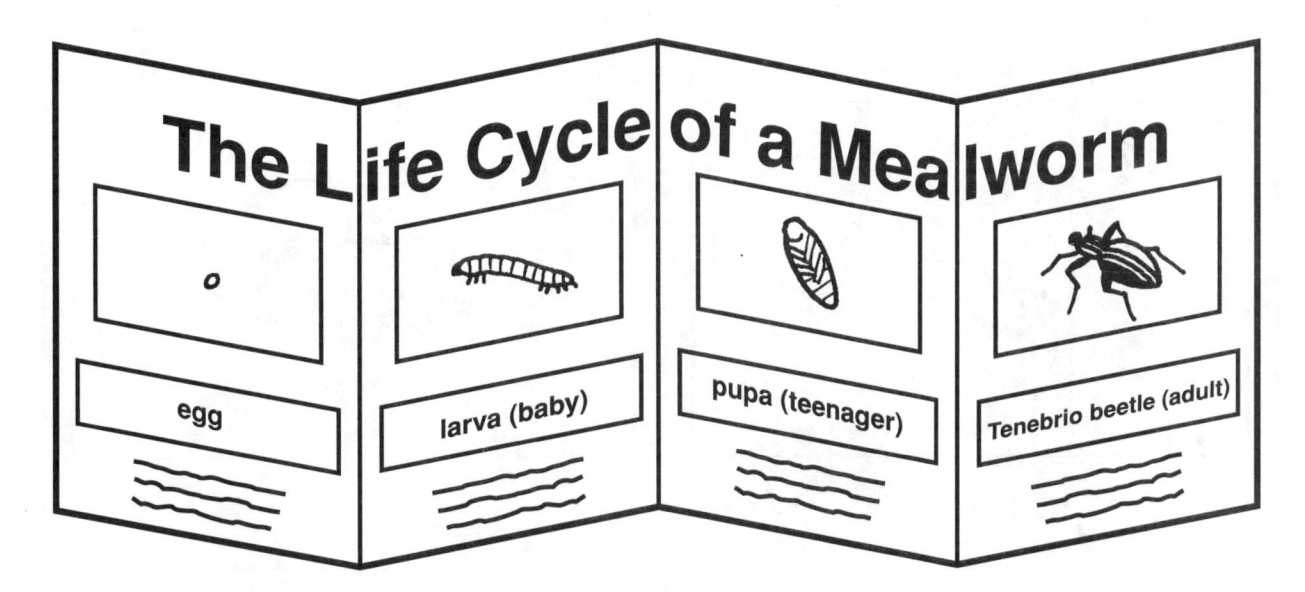

2. Cut apart the four boxes on page 44 and paste them onto each section of the construction paper to show the life cycle of a mealworm. Label each picture. Color the pictures.

3. Write your own information about each stage. Share your life cycle facts with a friend.

Mealworms

Magnificent Mealworms *(cont.)*

See page 43 for suggested use.

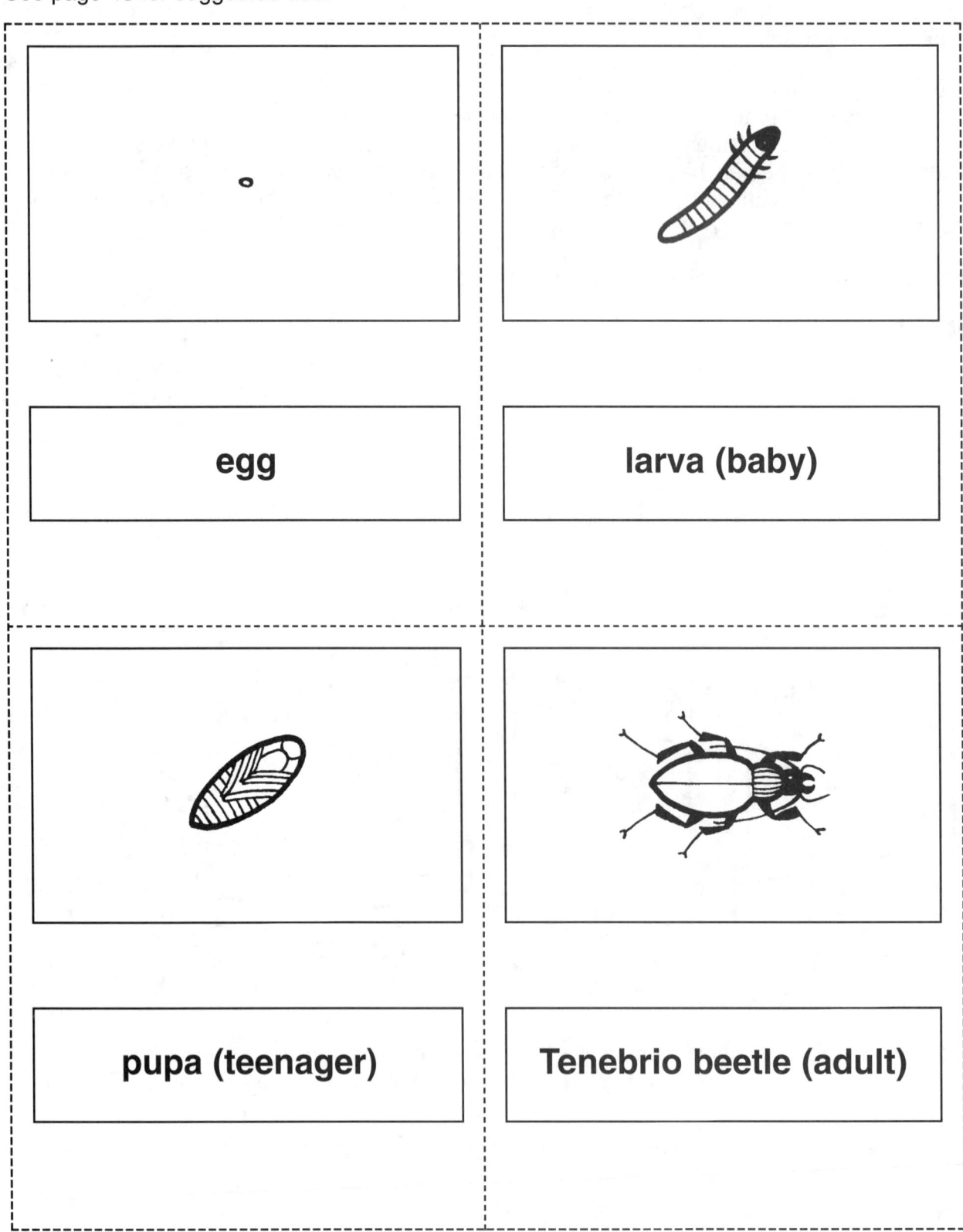

egg	larva (baby)

pupa (teenager)	Tenebrio beetle (adult)

Language Arts

Journal Entry Questions

Create journals for each child by taking writing/drawing paper appropriate to your children's level and binding the pages in a homemade construction paper, or purchased, folder. Let your children enjoy decorating the front cover by drawing free-hand illustrations, using reproduced journal covers (page 46), or by providing copies of the clip art (page 78) to be colored, cut out and pasted on the cover.

You may choose to utilize the journals as part of the learning process each day or only as time permits. The journal entry questions below are suggestions only. The questions may be used in conjunction with a presented lesson or as a "Question of the Day." Encourage your children to respond in their journals with illustrations, as well as words and/or sentences.

1. What is the name of your silkworm/mealworm? Describe it and draw it in detail. Is it the same or different from the other silkworms/mealworms?
2. What does it feel like to touch a silkworm/mealworm?
3. What do you like about silkworms/mealworms? What do you not like about silkworms and/or mealworms?
4. Do you think silkworms/mealworms would make good pets? Why or why not?
5. What things now remind you of a silkworm/mealworm?
6. How does it feel when you hold a silkworm/mealworm in your hand?
7. What does silk feel like? What do I wish was made of silk?
8. Silkworms/mealworms are constantly growing. How tall would you like to be? Why?
9. What has been or is your favorite part about studying silkworms/mealworms?

Challenge: Have your children take turns making up a journal entry question for the day. This is an excellent way to assess if the children are truly assimilating their new knowledge.

Life Cycle Journal Pages

You may want to add extra pages at the end of the journals for children to document the life cycle changes observed with their own silkworm and mealworm. Have the children draw illustrations and label them each day to record the small changes their silkworm and mealworm makes.

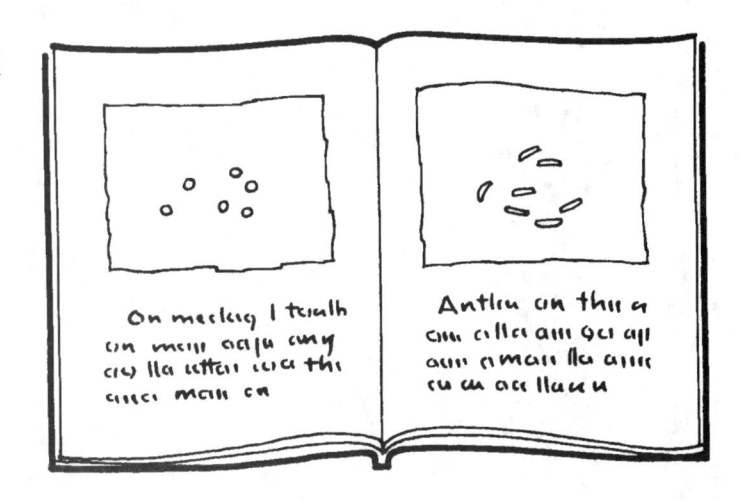

Language Arts

Journal Cover

_____ Journal

Language Arts

Create-a-Sentence

A sentence is made up of a string of certain kinds of words. A sentence must have at least one subject (noun) and one verb (action). Choose one word or group of words from each list to create a sentence. Write your sentence on the line and then illustrate it. (Don't forget to punctuate!)

Noun	Verb	Second Noun (optional)
The mealworm	squirms	silk
A silkworm	eats	a cocoon
A caterpillar	spins	bran
A beetle	flies	skin
The moth	molts	leaves
The egg	sleeps	

_____

_____

My Illustration

Language Arts

Poetry Page

Tongue Twisters

Tongue twisters are a string of words that all begin with the same letter or sound.

Slinky Sam saw skinny silkworms stuck on a stem.

Now make one up. Have a friend try to say it fast three times!

_____

_____

Haiku

Japanese Haiku poems are three lines in length. The first line has five syllables; the second, seven; and the third, five.

Silkworms squirming fast.
Growing and always changing.
Spinning strands of silk.

Try one of your own.

_____

_____

Title-Down Poetry

Title-down poetry is a form of poetry in which the letters that spell the subject of the poem are used as the beginning of each line. Read the poem below. Then write your own title-down poem about a worm.

Try one.

Silkworms	W _____
In cocoons	O _____
Love to spin the	R _____
King's future silk pajamas!	M _____

#2371 Thematic Unit—Silkworms and Mealworms © Teacher Created Materials, Inc.

Language Arts

A Day in the Life of a Silkworm

See page 19, #3 for suggested use.

1	2
3	4

Math

Silkworm Scavenger Hunt

Search and see if you can find things that are like a silkworm in weight, height, size, length, and color.

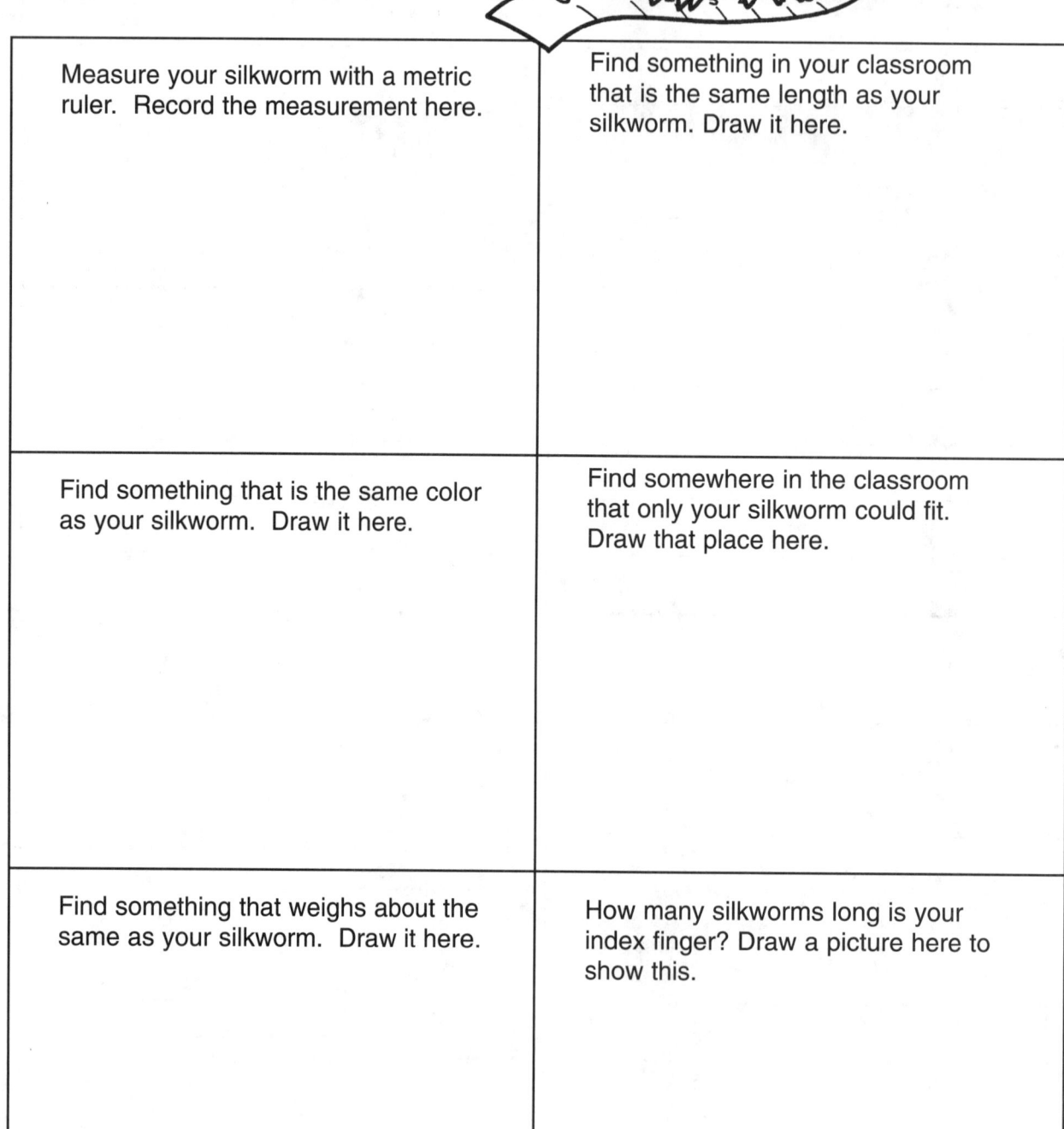

Measure your silkworm with a metric ruler. Record the measurement here.	Find something in your classroom that is the same length as your silkworm. Draw it here.
Find something that is the same color as your silkworm. Draw it here.	Find somewhere in the classroom that only your silkworm could fit. Draw that place here.
Find something that weighs about the same as your silkworm. Draw it here.	How many silkworms long is your index finger? Draw a picture here to show this.

Math

Place Value Practice

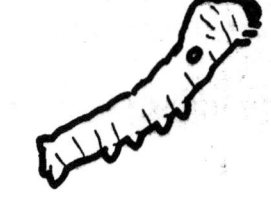

🦋 = 10   🐛 = 1

What number does the moths and silkworms represent?

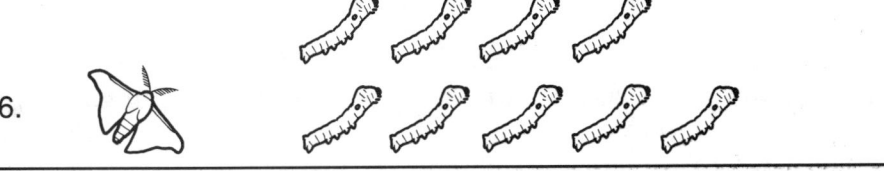

1. 🦋🦋🦋 🐛🐛 = _____

2. 🦋🦋🦋🦋🦋 = _____

3. 🦋🦋 🐛🐛🐛🐛🐛 = _____

4. 🦋🦋🦋🦋 🐛🐛 = _____

5. 🦋🦋🦋🦋 🐛🐛🐛🐛 = _____

6. 🦋 🐛🐛🐛🐛🐛🐛🐛🐛🐛 = _____

© Teacher Created Materials, Inc.   51   #2371 Thematic Unit—Silkworms and Mealworms

Math

Mealworm Mania

Q: Why would a mealworm wear tennies?

Directions: Add the numbers in each shoe. Find the sum in the code box and color the shoe by using the code.

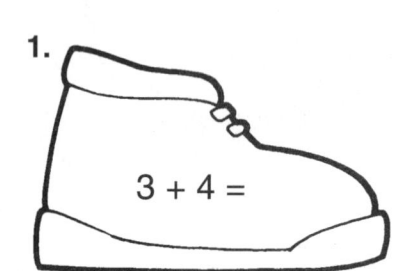

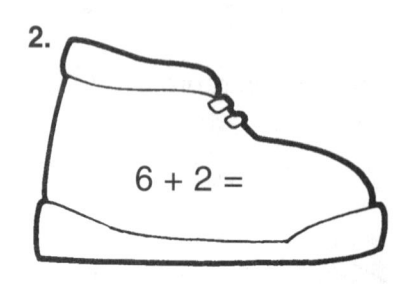

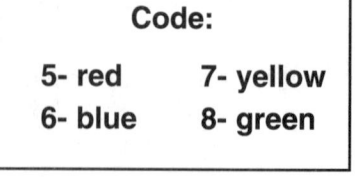

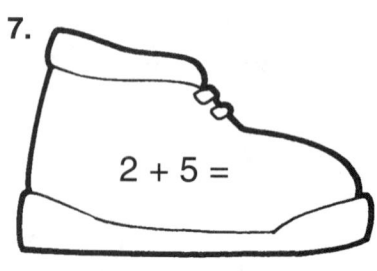

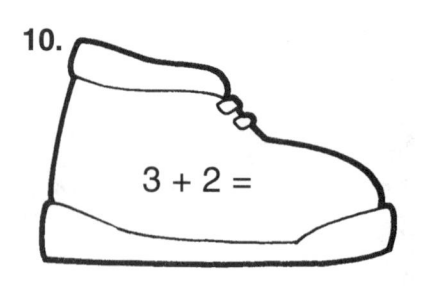

Code:
5- red   7- yellow
6- blue 8- green

1. $3 + 4 =$
2. $6 + 2 =$
3. $3 + 3 =$
4. $1 + 4 =$
5. $4 + 4 =$
6. $2 + 4 =$
7. $2 + 5 =$
8. $4 + 3 =$
9. $3 + 5 =$
10. $3 + 2 =$

A: Because 'ninies' are too small and 'elevenies' are too big.

Challenge: If a mealworm really wore tennis shoes (one per foot), how many shoes would it need?

Science

Beetle Mania

Roll the die to see which part of the Tenebrio beetle to draw first, second, third, fourth, fifth, and sixth. Use the key to help you draw your beetle. It might take a lot of rolls before you are finished!

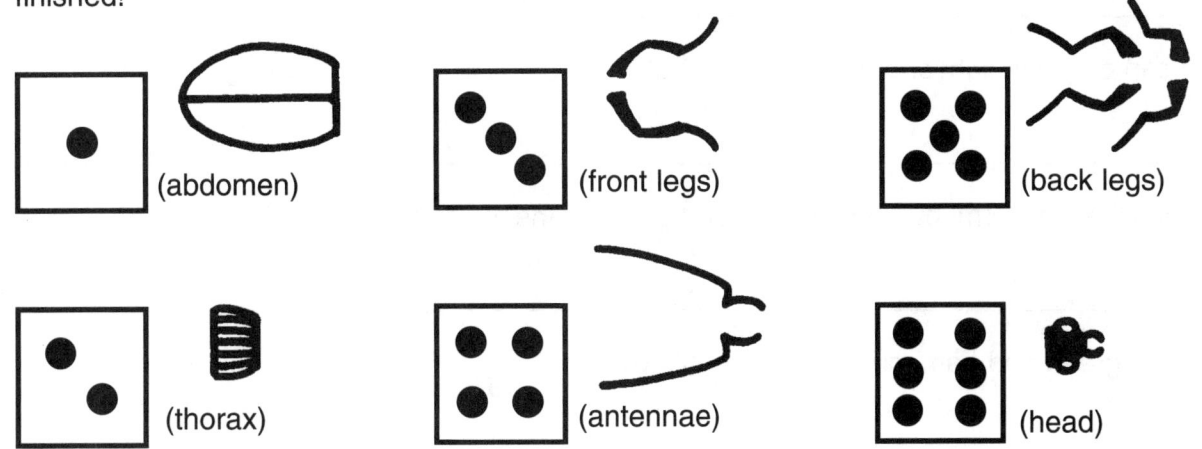

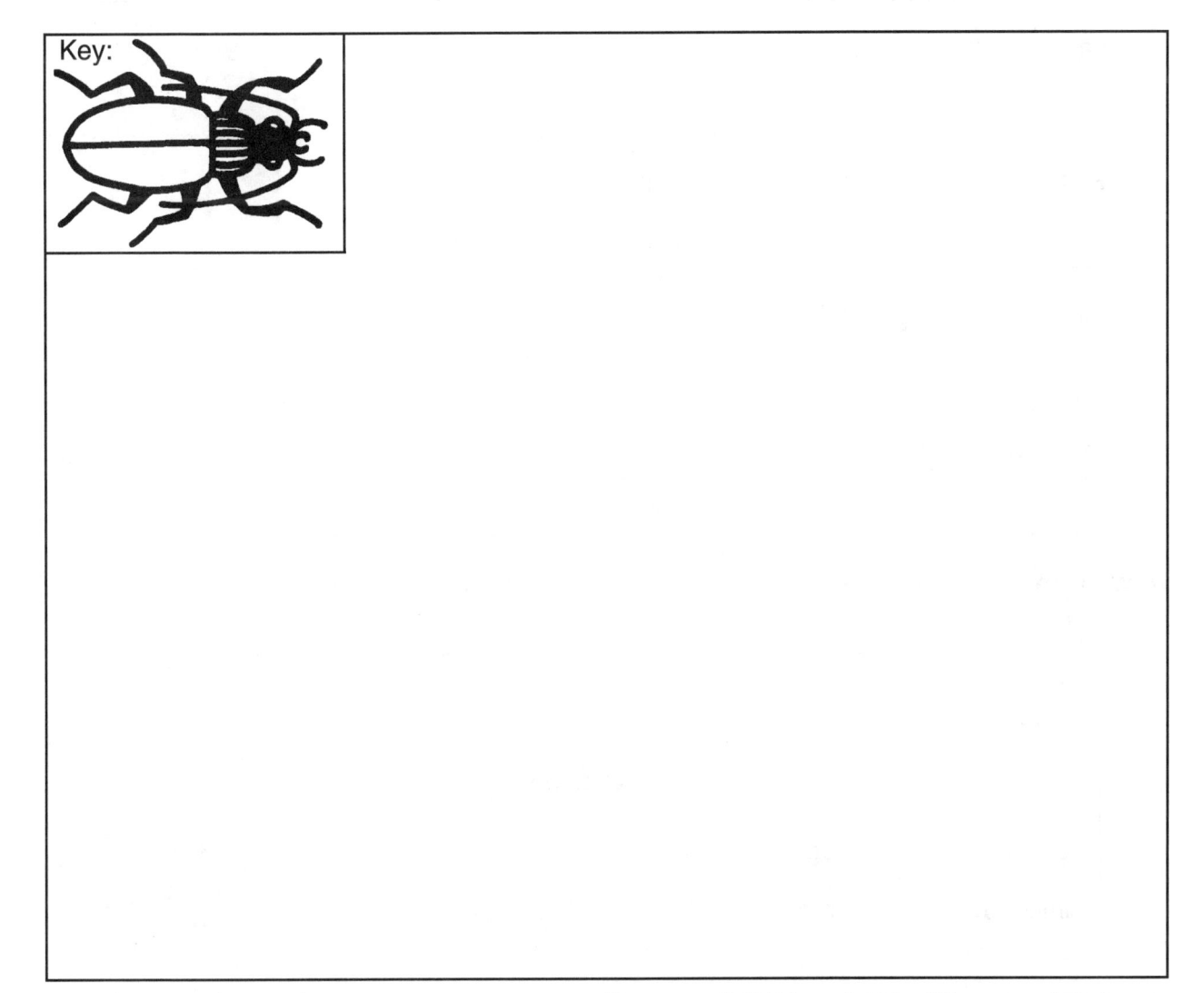

- ⚀ (abdomen)
- ⚂ (front legs)
- ⚄ (back legs)
- ⚁ (thorax)
- ⚃ (antennae)
- ⚅ (head)

Key:

Science

What am I? Riddles

1. I have a hairy body with feathery antennae.
   _____

2. I can only see light and dark images.
   _____

3. I look like a worm, but I am the second stage of the life cycle.
   _____

4. I am green and I am munched on by silkworms.
   _____

5. I am as tiny as the head of a pin. I am yellowish.
   _____

6. Snug in a cocoon of silk, I begin to change again.
   _____

7. Silk comes through me from the silkworm's body.
   _____

8. I am made from one long, long strand of silk.
   _____

Now make up your own riddle and see if a friend can solve it:
   _____

Word Box

cocoon	egg	spinneret	larva
simple eye	moth	Mulberry leaf	pupa

Science

What is a Worm?

Mealworms and silkworms are not really worms. They are caterpillars. Caterpillars have little legs and antennae. They change into bugs, butterflies, and moths.

Circle the caterpillars. Put an **X** on the worms. Color the mealworm brown. Color the silkworm yellow.

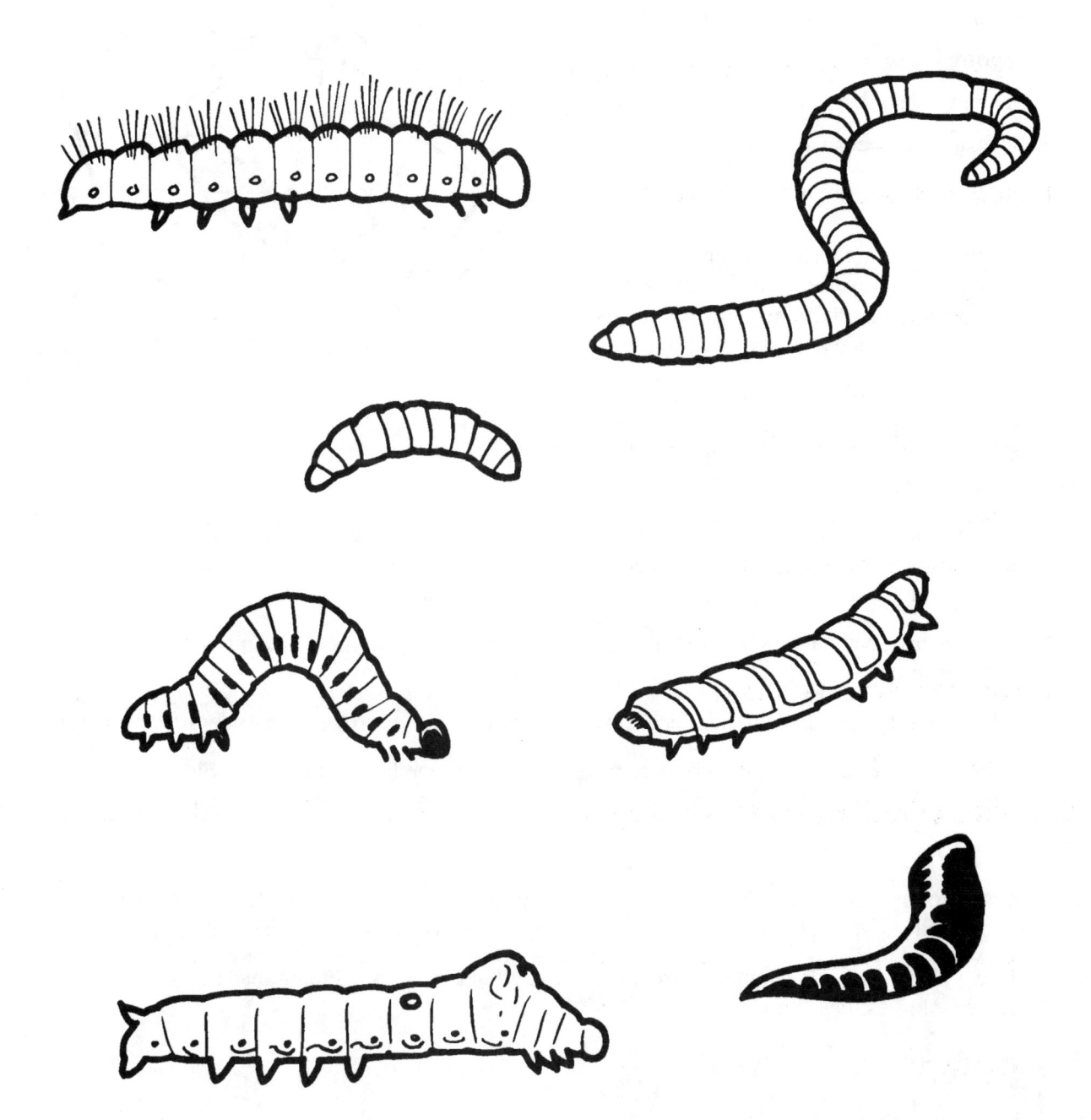

© Teacher Created Materials, Inc.   #2371 Thematic Unit—Silkworms and Mealworms

Science

How Strong is Silk?

The secret of silk being woven into clothing was kept for hundreds of years. Women used to wear silk stockings, but now panty hose are made with synthetic (man-made) materials such as nylon.

Materials Needed (for groups of four children)

- four 12" (30 cm) strands of silk thread
- four 12" (30 cm) strands of polyester thread
- a spring scale
- an empty metal key ring
- data capture sheet (page 57)

Procedure

1. Ask the children which they think is stronger, silk thread or polyester thread. Have them share their hypotheses. Place the children into groups of four and provide each group with needed supplies.

2. Ask the groups to tie one end of a silk thread to the end of the spring scale and tie the other end of the silk thread to the key ring.

3. Ask one child to hold the spring scale while another child holds the key ring. A third child stands ready to watch the pointer of the scale to see at which degree on the scale the thread breaks. A fourth child is ready to record the results on the group's data capture sheet.

4. After reaching a result with the silk thread, have the groups repeat the procedure with the polyester thread.

5. If time permits, have the children repeat each experiment with each thread a total of four times.

6. Gather together all the groups and share the results. Make one large class graph. Find the average of the breaking degree for both the silk and polyester threads. Formulate a class conclusion.

Bonus Ideas

1. In their journals, have the children draw a picture of a piece of silk clothing they have designed for themselves. Have them describe how it would make them feel to wear it.

2. Have a "Wear Silk" day in the classroom where everyone wears something made of silk (i.e. scarves, blouses, ties, etc.).

Science

How Strong is Silk? (cont.)

Data Capture Sheet

Record how much pull it took to break each type of thread. Then answer the questions below.

Testing Pull	Silk	Polyester
Test 1		
Test 2		
Test 3		
Test 4		
Average Degree of Pull		

What type of thread do you believe is stronger? Why?

_____

_____

_____

Did you notice anything about the way in which either strand broke? Explain.

_____

_____

_____

Social Studies

Producers of Silk Map

Use the map and map key to fill in the blanks.

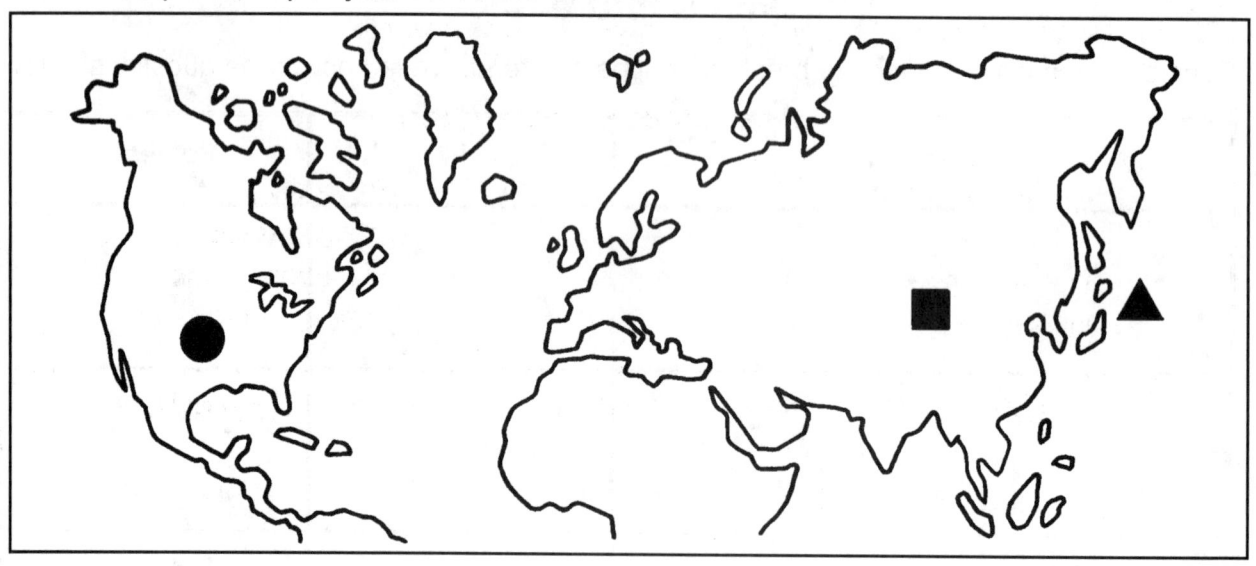

Key:
● United States   ▲ Japan   ■ China
🧵 silk   🐛 Silkworms

1. _____ 🐛 were first discovered to make silk in _____ ■ .

2. _____ ▲ is now the biggest exporter of silk.

3. We live in the _____ ● .

4. _____ 🧵 has to travel a long way to get to where we live.

5. Draw a path on your map from where _____ 🧵 is made in _____ ▲ and to the _____ ● where we wear clothes made from _____ 🐛 .

#2371 Thematic Unit—Silkworms and Mealworms   58   © Teacher Created Materials, Inc.

Social Studies

Some Creepy Crawlies Help Us

Silkworms are helpful to humans. The silk they spin can be woven into beautiful pieces of clothing. Many insects are helpful to humans, but some are harmful.

Some creepy crawlies...

- pollinate plants
- make honey
- provide beauty
- eat harmful insects

- bite or sting
- carry diseases
- ruin crops, plants
- damage clothes, food

Helpful	Both	Harmful

✂ Cut and paste.

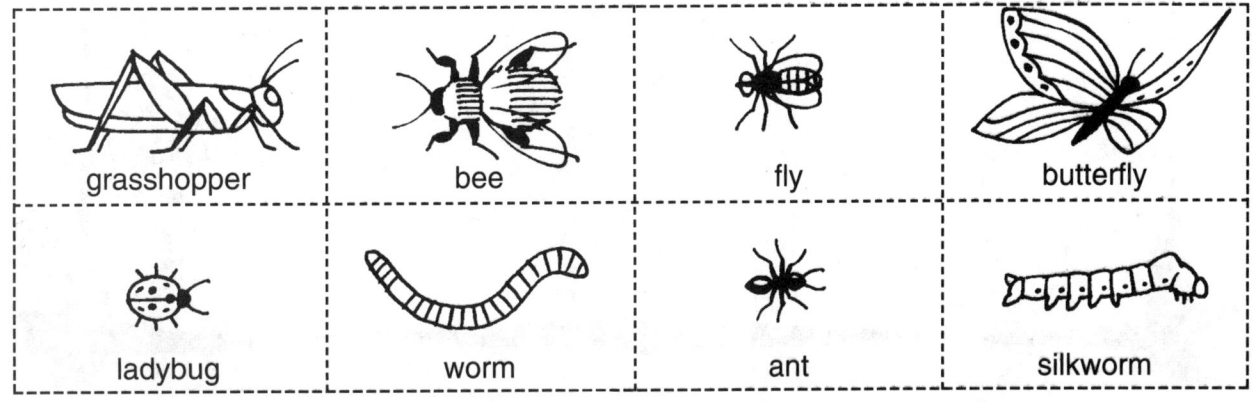

grasshopper	bee	fly	butterfly
ladybug	worm	ant	silkworm

Art

See-a-Scene

Draw a picture from the story *The Empress and the Silkworm* in the box below.

Art

Spin a Cocoon

Materials
- string
- liquid starch
- empty toilet paper tube
- tempera paints
- paint brushes

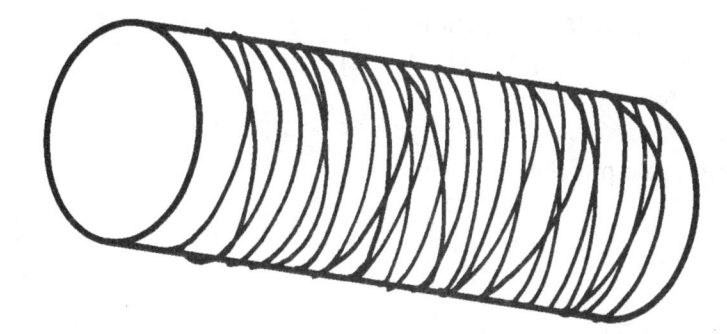

Directions

1. Dip the string in the liquid starch and then wrap the string around and around the paper tube; allow it to dry.
2. Paint the cocoon with tempera paint; allow the cocoon to dry.

Tissue Paper Moth

Materials
- tan cardstock
- pencil
- scissors
- brown, tan, white tissue art paper
- dilluted liquid starch
- paint brushes
- moth pattern (below)

Directions

1. Trace the moth pattern onto cardstock with a pencil; cut the pattern out.
2. Using small pieces of tissue paper, place a few at a time onto the traced moth silhouette. Brush a thin coat of liquid starch over tissue pieces; repeat until the moth is covered. Allow it to dry. Place the moth inside the prepared cocoon (directions above).

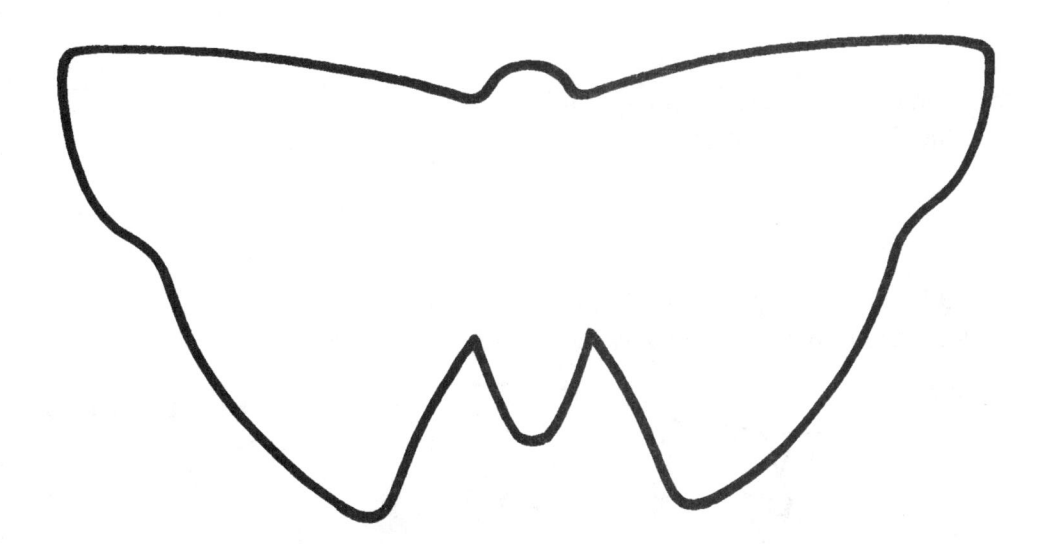

Art

Creepy Crawly Mealworm

Materials (per child)

- 5 empty toilet paper tubes, cut into three equal sections each (Each child will use 13 sections.)
- tan or light brown tempera and paintbrush
- 24 brad fasteners per child
- scissors
- small-hole hole puncher
- glue

Directions

1. Cut a rounded notch out of each side of each end of the toilet paper roll's cut sections.

2. Punch two holes next to the notched edges of the rolls.

Steps 1 and 2

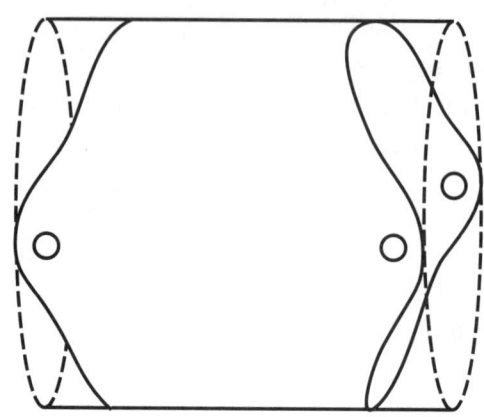

3. Provide each child with 13 prepared sections. Have the children paint each section; dry the sections thoroughly.

Step 4

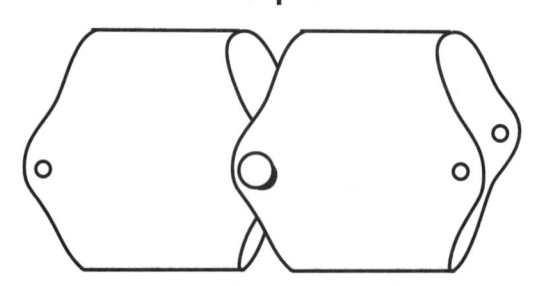

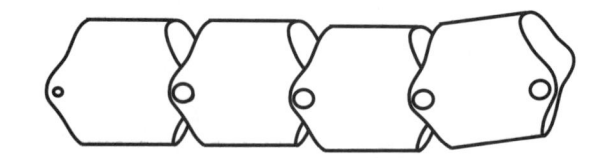

4. Connect the toilet paper tube sections by inserting a brad fastener in one hole of one toilet paper tube and through the matching hole in the next tube (See step 4 illustrations.) Spread fasteners apart to hold the tubes in place. The sections should be able to swivel slightly.

5. Cut out legs and eyes from the toilet paper tube remnants. Glue them to the caterpillar, as shown.

6. Allow the children to finish painting their mealworms by painting the eyes and legs with tempera paints; allow the paint to dry and display the completed mealworms.

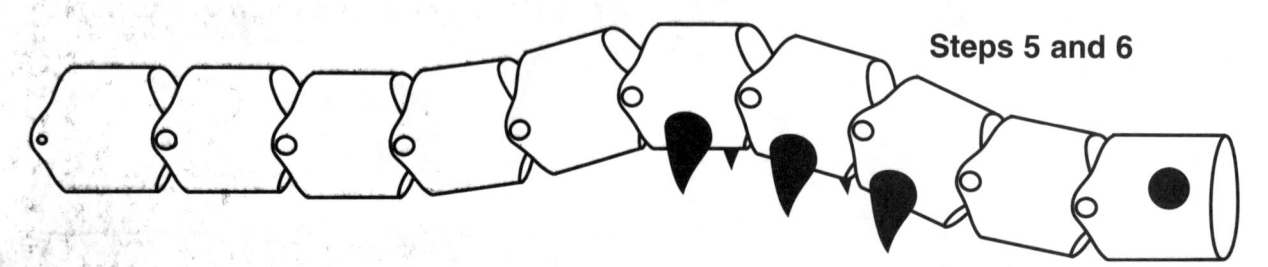

Steps 5 and 6

#2371 Thematic Unit—Silkworms and Mealworms

Drama

Popsicle Puppets

Use the patterns below for the children to make puppets. Reproduce patterns onto cardstock. Cut out, color, and laminate. Attach patterns to popsicle sticks by gluing or stapling. Have the children put on their own puppet shows about the silkworm's life cycle.

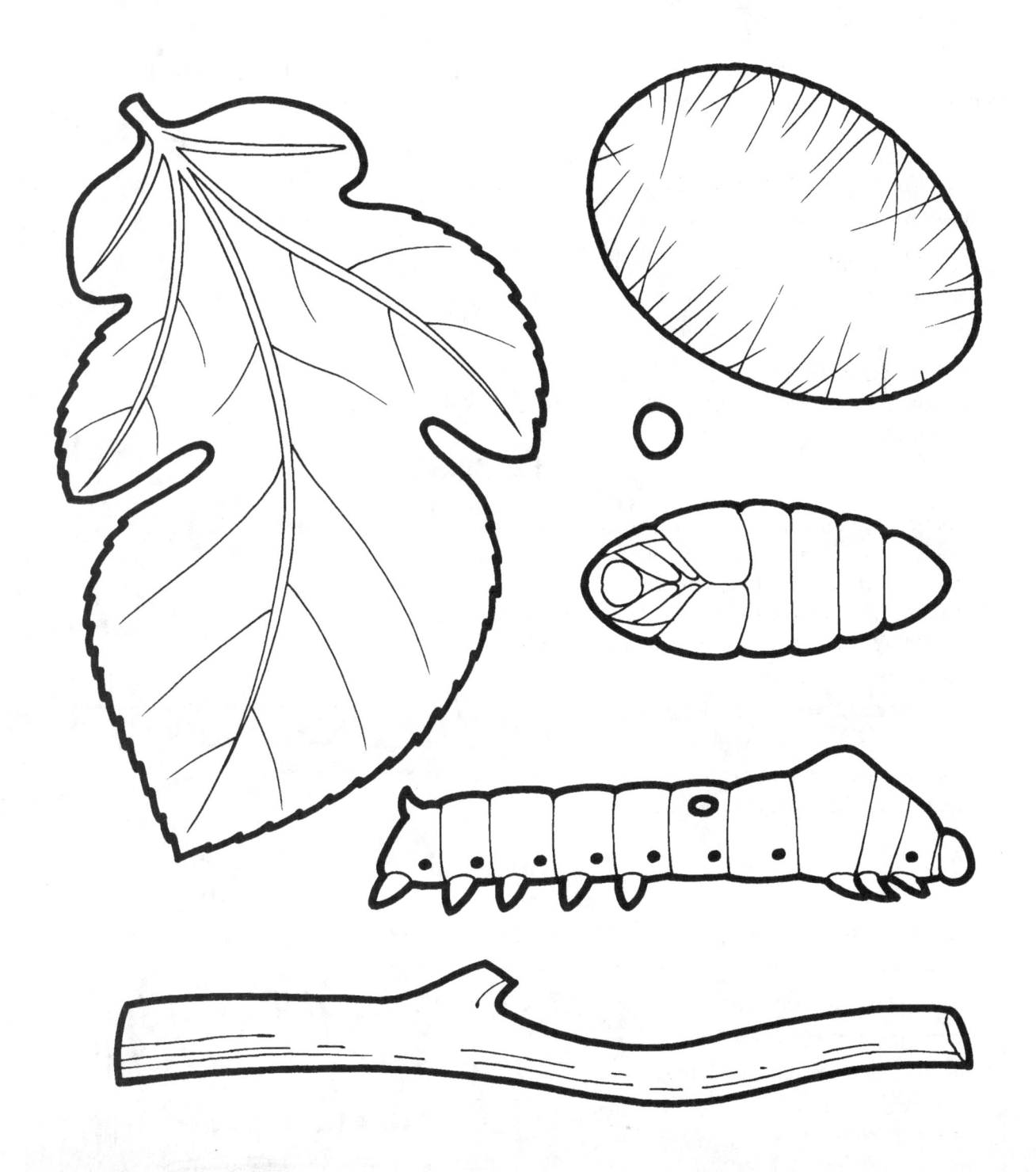

Music

Wormy Musical Songs

The Worms Are...
(To the tune of *The Ants Go Marching*)

The silkworms are spinning one by one, hurrah! Hurrah!
The silkworms are spinning one by one, hurrah! Hurrah!
The silkworms are spinning one by one, the little one stops to spin some silk, and they all go spinning 'round and 'round and 'round! Spin! Spin! Spin! . . .

The silkworms are squirming one by one, hurrah! Hurrah!
The silkworms are squirming one by one, hurrah! Hurrah!
The silkworms are squirming one by one, the little one pop out of its cocoon, and they all go squirming to get right out of their skin! Squirm! Squirm! Squirm! . . .

The mealworms are munching one by one, hurrah! Hurrah!
The mealworms are munching one by one, hurrah! Hurrah!
The mealworms are munching one by one, the little one stops to chomp some bran, and they all go marching to eat up all the grains! Munch! Munch! Munch! . . .

Teeny-Tiny Silkworm
(To the tune of *Itsy Bitsy Spider*)

Teeny-tiny silkworm crawled up onto a leaf,
Spun his cocoon and slept so quietly.
Inside his cocoon he didn't make a sound.
He dreamt of his new life when he'd be flying around.
While he was sleeping the snow did gently fall,
Winter came and went then he heard the robin call,
"Come out Mr. Moth, come out of your cocoon.
Spread your wings and fly for me
While I sing my little tune."

The Munching Silkworm
(To the tune of *Twinkle, Twinkle, Little Star*)

Munching, munching, little worm,
Munching, munching, watch you squirm.
Munching on a Mulberry leaf,
Munching, munching, eat, eat, eat!
Munching, munching, all day through,
Munching is so fun to do!

Music

Wormy Musical Songs *(cont.)*

Where is...?
(To the tune of *Where is Thumpkin?*)

Where is mealworm?
Where is mealworm?
Here I am,
Eating bran.

How are you today, sir?
Very well, I thank you,
Yummy bran! Yummy bran!

Where is silkworm?
Where is silkworm?
Here I am,
Eating leaves.

How are you today, sir?
Very well, I thank you.
Yummy leaves! Yummy leaves!

Five Small Mealworms

(Can be presented as a finger play or sung to the tune of *Twinkle, Twinkle, Little Star*)

Five small mealworms, sitting in a row,
(Hold up one hand and wiggle fingers.)

First one said, "We really have to go,"
(Shake your pointer finger.)

Second one said, "Let's go and find some bran."
(Put hand above eyebrows and look around.)

The third one said, "Squirm as fast as you can."
(Put palms of hands together and wiggle hands back and forth.)

The fourth one said, "Let's munch and munch and munch."
(Make chomping motion with hands.)

And the fifth one said, "I'm ready for some lunch!"
(Rub your tummy and say, "Mmmmmmmm.")

© Teacher Created Materials, Inc. #2371 Thematic Unit—Silkworms and Mealworms

Life Skills

Cooking with Bran

Mealworms aren't the only ones that like to eat bran and cornmeal. Let's add some ingredients to bran and cornmeal and see what you can make. Make sure an older person helps you in the kitchen so you will be safe.

Bran Chocolate Clusters

Ingredients
- 1 package (6 ounces or 150 g) semisweet chocolate chips
- ⅓ cup (85 mL) margarine or butter
- 16 large marshmallows
- ½ tsp (2.5 mL) vanilla
- 1 cup (236 mL) oats
- ½ cup (125 mL) bran cereal
- 1 cup (236 mL) flaked coconut

Directions
Heat chocolate chips, margarine, and marshmallows in a sauce pan over low heat, stirring constantly until smooth; remove from heat. Mix in vanilla, oats, bran cereal, and coconut. Drop mixture by teaspoonfuls onto waxed paper and shape into clusters with hands. Refrigerate until firm, about 30 minutes. Makes about 40 clusters.

Corn Meal Muffins

Ingredients
- 1 ½ cups (354 ml) cornmeal
- ½ cup (118 mL) all-purpose flour
- 2 tsp. (10 mL) baking powder
- 1 tsp. (5 mL) sugar
- 1 tsp. (5 mL) salt
- ½ tsp. (2.5 mL) baking soda
- ¼ cup (59 mL) shortening
- 1 ½ cups (354 mL) buttermilk
- 2 eggs

Directions
Heat oven to 450 degrees F (230 degrees C). Mix all ingredients in a large bowl; beat vigorously 30 seconds. Fill 14 greased medium muffin cups about ¾ full. Bake about 20 minutes. Cool completely on a cooling rack.

Culminating Activities

Culmination Games

The following activities can be used at the end of each lesson or at the end of the unit. You will need to adapt the activities according to whether you are reviewing silkworms or mealworms.

Sixty Seconds

Place the children into groups of three. Using a stop watch or clock to time one minute, have one child be the timekeeper, another be the listener, and the third be on the "hot seat." (Have the children take turns with all three of the roles.) The person on the "hot seat" has sixty seconds to say all that he or she knows about the subject being assessed. The timekeeper lets the "hot seat" child know when to begin and stop. While groups are playing the game, move around the room and listen to what the children are saying.

Draw the Picture

Divide your classroom into groups of three or four. Provide each group with their own drawing paper and crayons. Make certain that the players (children in each group) cannot see each other's paper or drawings (within their own group). One child in each group is chosen to be the leader. The leader describes a picture generated in his or her mind while he or she and the rest of the group tries to draw what they hear being described by the leader. (The picture needs to be something related to silkworms or mealworms.) When the drawings are finished, everyone holds up his or her picture. This is a great activity to increase listening skills, as well as tickling the funnybone!

Pass The Word

Divide your classroom into groups of five or six. Give each group a word, i.e. silkworm, mealworm, metamorphosis, etc. The first player in the group then says a word that has to do something with the original word. The next player must say a related word to the second word mentioned. The players carry on around the group saying a newly related word until one of them cannot think of a new word or someone repeats an already spoken word. This person is "out." The last child to have said an approved word gets to choose the new word and the game continues.

Culminating Activities

Show What You Know

Draw a line from the word to the correct picture.

antennae

Tenebrio beetle

egg

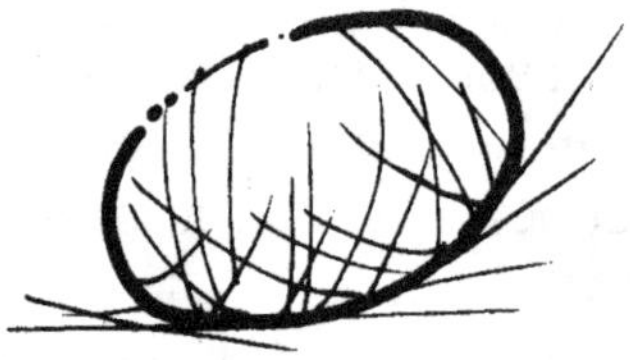

larva

pupa

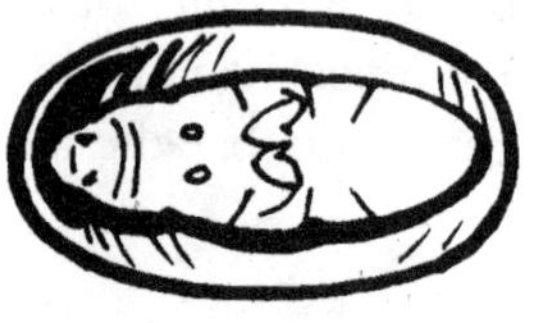

cocoon

silkworm moth

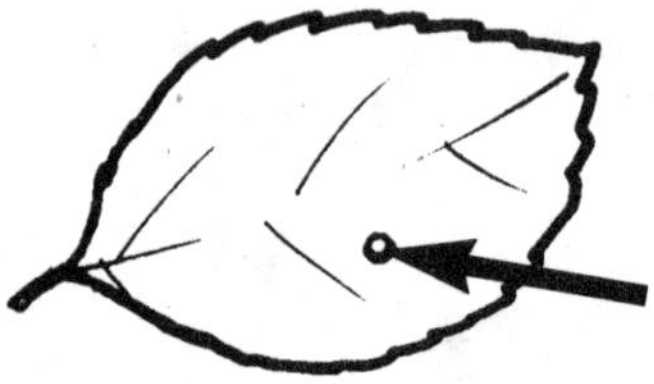

Unit Management

Silkworm and Mealworm Habitats

Studying silkworms and mealworms can help the children gain an understanding and appreciation for living things around them.

Silkworms

Materials

- clear plastic or glass container
- Mulberry leaves (cleaned well with warm water and very mild solution of soap; dry thoroughly)
- empty egg cartons (cut the tops off and discard)
- dark construction paper or newspaper (wrap around outside of jar to create a darkened environment)

Directions

Silkworms must have fresh Mulberry leaves constantly available in their habitat for food. Remove old leaves before adding freshly cleaned ones. Do not put the silkworms or cocoons near any kind of water (they will get all the moisture they need from the leaves themselves). Periodically remove the outer paper wrapping to gain a better view of the silkworms and cocoons. After viewing replace the dark covering. You do not need to place a netting over the mouth of the container; silkworm moths cannot fly!

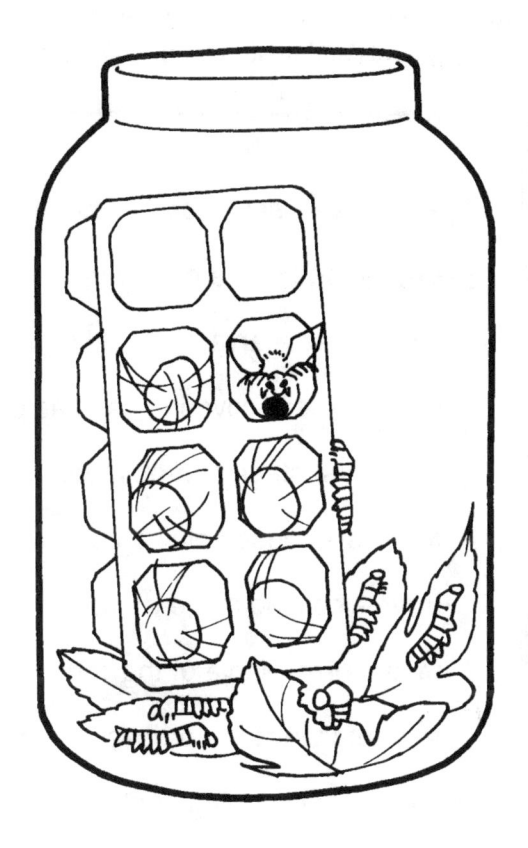

Mealworms

Materials

- plastic, glass, or metal container with slick sides (recycled margarine containers work well)
- bran flakes
- apple, carrot, or potato pieces
- damp cloth
- rubber band

Directions

Put a small handful or two of bran in bottom of the container. Add a few pieces of fruit or vegetable for moisture. Add three or four mealworms to the habitat. Place a damp cloth over the top; secure it with a rubber band. Replace the food as needed.

Three Important Safety Rules

1. Silkworms and mealworms are living things, always handle them gently.
2. Mealworms need to be kept at the appropriate temperatures (see Culturing Mealworms, page 28).
3. When doing experiments, silkworms and mealworms must be watched at all times so they do not fall and become injured.

© Teacher Created Materials, Inc.

Unit Management

Silkworm and Mealworm Vocabulary

Use the following vocabulary words to help teach your children about the silkworm and the mealworm. Children should become familiar with what these words mean in their own words. Write these words on index cards and post them in your classroom so your children become familiar with them.

antennae—sense organs on the head that respond to touch and odor

bran—food of the mealworm

caterpillar—larva of a silkworm moth

cocoon—silk covering used as protection during pupa development

egg—first stage of metamorphosis

instars—period between a silkworm larva's molts

larva—second stage of metamorphosis

mealworm—larva of the Tenebrio beetle

metamorphosis—process of changing in the life cycle of most insects

molting—shedding of old skin and growing new skin

Mulberry leaf—food of the silkworm

pupa—third stage of metamorphosis

silk glands—organs in the silkworm's body that produce silk

silkworm—larva of a silkworm moth

Silkworm moth—final stage of the silkworm

simple eye—an eye only able to determine light and dark

spinneret—tube on silkworm's head that the silk comes through

Tenebrio beetle—final stage of the mealworm

Letters to Parents

Dear Parents,

We are about to embark on the study of silkworms and mealworms. Studying these creatures can help your child gain an understanding and appreciation for living things.

New vocabulary will be learned in class. Be prepared to talk to your child at home about these new words and what they mean. Some of the vocabulary words for this unit are: metamorphosis, life cycle, egg, larva, pupa, silkworm, silkworm moth, mealworm, and Tenebrio beetle.

This unit will feature two highly acclaimed books (*Silkworms* and *The Empress and the Silkworm*) to help children understand and learn about the silkworms. We invite you to read these books, too. They are available at most public libraries and bookstores.

We have set up a Silkworm and Mealworm Research Center in our room that has been filled with books and other materials to aid in our study. We would like to enlist your help and support in our efforts. We are looking for guest speakers and additional materials you may have on this subject. Please contact me if you have any information or materials.

We appreciate your help in making our study of silkworms and mealworms a success!

Sincerely yours,

_____

Dear Parents,

Tomorrow we will be doing an experiment with mealworms to find out what they might like to eat. We need each child to bring in an item that he or she thinks a mealworm might like to eat. The sample of food needs to be small since mealworms are very tiny. Please send the bit of food in a small sealed plastic bag with your child's name on it.

If you have any questions, please do not hesitate to call me at school.

Sincerely yours,

_____

Unit Management

Bulletin Boards

The Silkworm Story

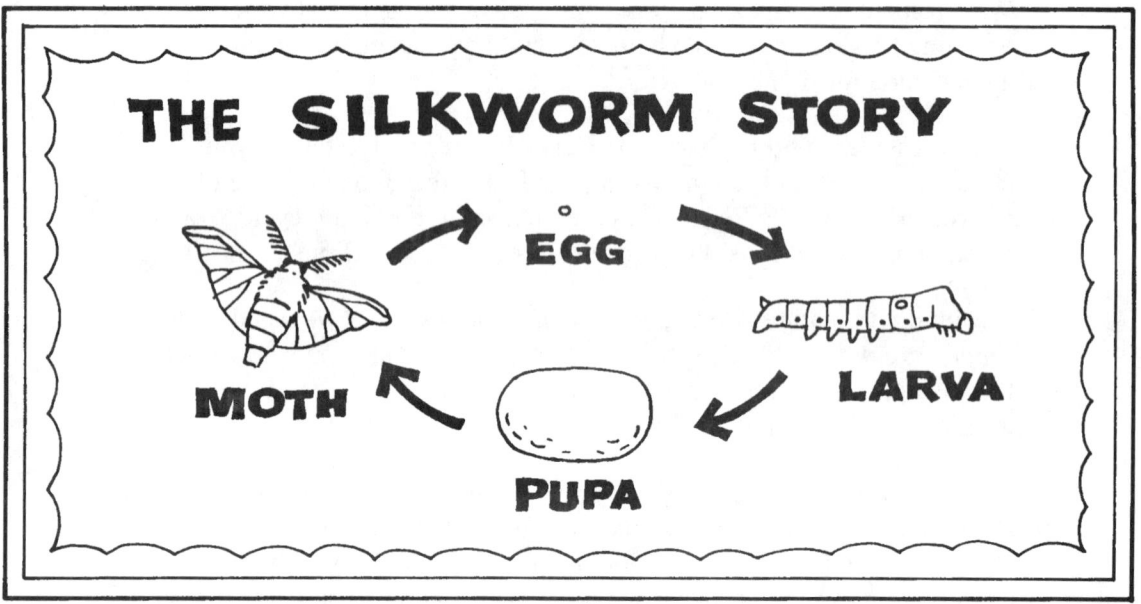

Cover the bulletin board with butcher paper or material. Add a border and the cut out letters: THE SILKWORM STORY. Post pictures of the egg, larva, pupa, and silkworm moth (see clip art, page 78). Cut out arrows from black construction paper and arrange them on the bulletin board as shown above.

Soft as Silk

Cover the bulletin board with butcher paper or material. Add a border and the cut out letters: SOFT AS SILK. Mount a map of the world and put cut out arrows with the word SILK written on them, pointing where silk is made (China and Japan). Hang different clothing items around the map that are made of silk.

Unit Management

Bulletin Boards *(cont.)*

Mealworm Mania T-Shirt

See page 25, #1 for suggested use.

Unit Management

Learning Centers

True or False

Using a science display board as a background, attach two library card holders, one on to the left side panel, the other on to the right side panel. Label: TRUE and FALSE. Add silkworm-related pictures to the display board. In a box labeled STATEMENTS, place informational statements about silkworms (some true and others false). If desired, you can change the statements daily. You can also assign a child to be a "teacher for the day" and write ten statements to go in the statements box. (Children can self-check their work, if desired, by writing the correct answer on the back of each statement.) Note: Simply change pictures on the display board from silkworms to mealworms when the subject has changed, along with providing appropriate mealworm true and false statements. This learning area can be used as a planned or free-time center.

Silk or Not Silk?

Using a science display board as a background, mount cut out letters: SILK or NOT SILK, and a variety of pictures of clothing cut out from magazines. Place two boxes in front of display board area. Label one SILK and the other NOT SILK. Put actual items of clothing on the table and have children determine whether they are made of silk or not. Those made of silk are placed in the SILK box, those not being placed in the NOT SILK box. (You may want to write the names or draw pictures of the clothing on the bottom of the boxes for self-checking purposes.)

Unit Management

Classroom Door Activities

Door Invitations

Door invitations are used to motivate the children towards active learning as they enter or exit doors. A door can serve as a "question asker," to share a fact that will spur interest, or as a review from yesterday's lessons. The key to door invitations is to change them often so children do not lose interest.

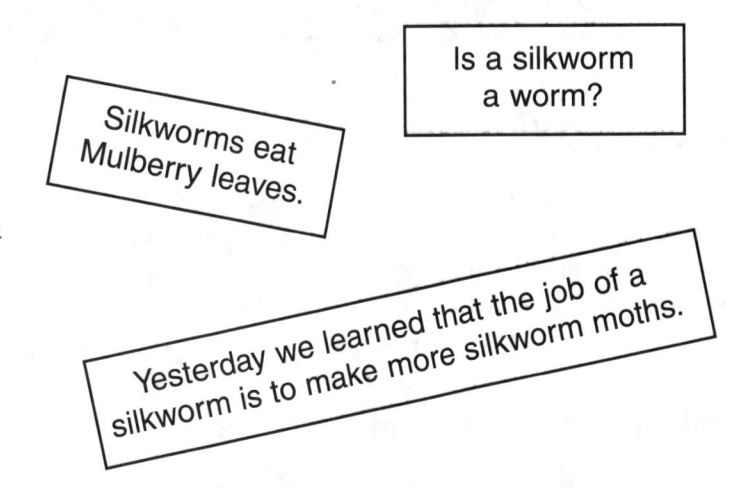

> Silkworms eat Mulberry leaves.

> Is a silkworm a worm?

> Yesterday we learned that the job of a silkworm is to make more silkworm moths.

Tracking My Silkworm's Life Cycle

On a large piece of white butcher paper taped over the door, draw the silkworm's life cycle stages (see page 13) and arrows on the white paper. Give children small self-sticking notes and have them write their names on the notes. All children place self-sticking notes in the egg area. As the children are observing their silkworms each day, have them place their personal sticky notes on the door's life cycle chart corresponding with the stage their silkworms are in.

For example, when a silkworm moves from an egg to larva, a child moves the note from the egg area to the larva area.

This serves as a great opportunity to see what all the silkworms are doing and that they can all be at different stages of growth.

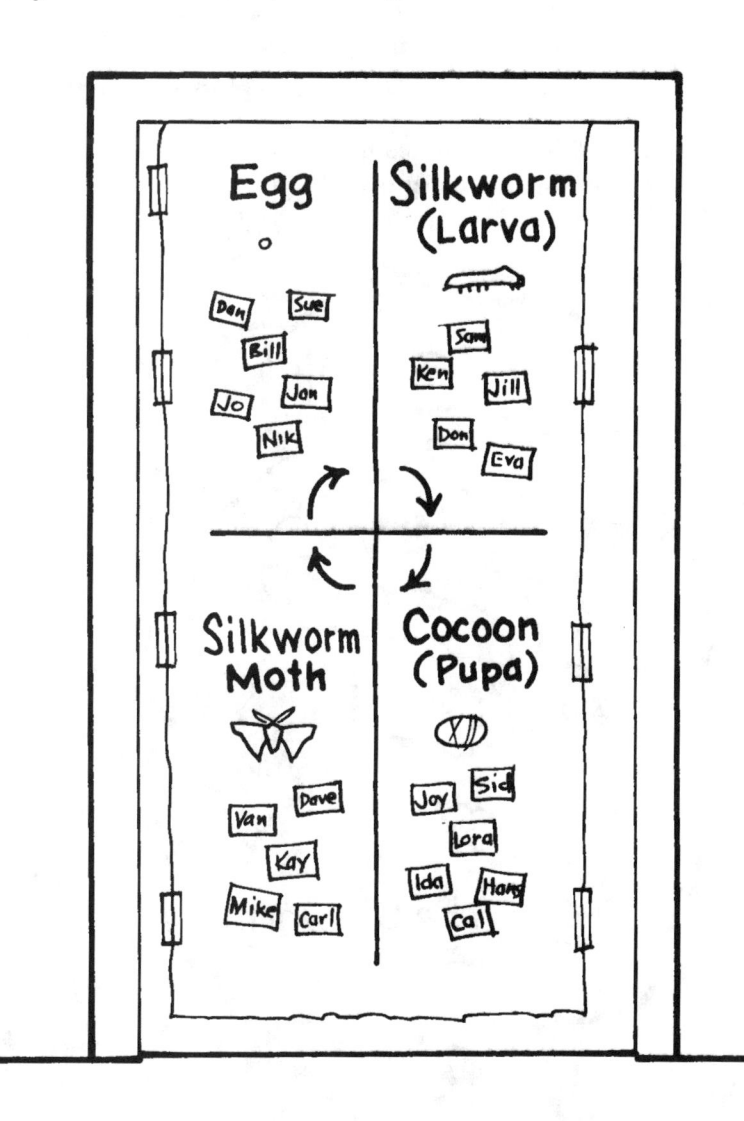

© Teacher Created Materials, Inc.   75   #2371 Thematic Unit—Silkworms and Mealworms

Unit Management

Behavioral Management Ideas

Silky, the Silkworm

To encourage the children to display good behavior, draw a large silkworm (clip art, page 78) using an opaque projector. Write "Silky, the Silkworm" on its body. Share with the children this incentive idea (or make up one of your own): Every time you see a child or group of children behaving appropriately you will add a sticker to Silky's body. Once its body is covered with stickers (or a predetermined number has been reached) you will provide a special classroom reward.

Dot-to-Dot Mealworm

Make a dot-to-dot mealworm. (You may want to simply adapt the silkworm pattern on page 23.) At the end of the day, discuss the class' behavior. If it was a good day, connect a dot, if not, simply do not connect a dot. Continue every day until the dot-to-dot mealworm is completely connected. Reward as desired.

Pencil Toppers

See page 27, # 6 for suggested uses. To make a pencil topper, cut out the shape, cut slits where indicated, and slip the topper over the pencil.

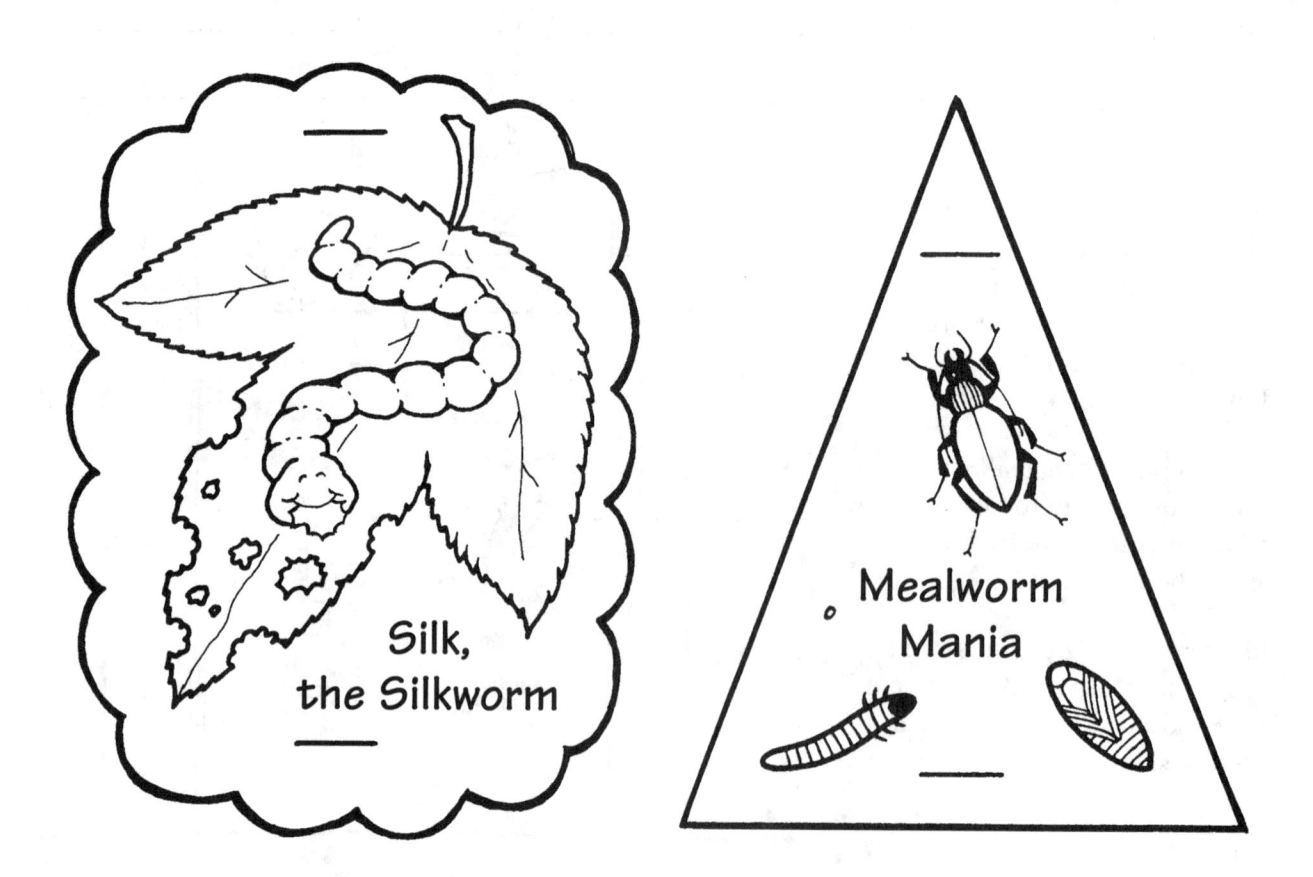

#2371 Thematic Unit—Silkworms and Mealworms © Teacher Created Materials, Inc.

Unit Management

Awards

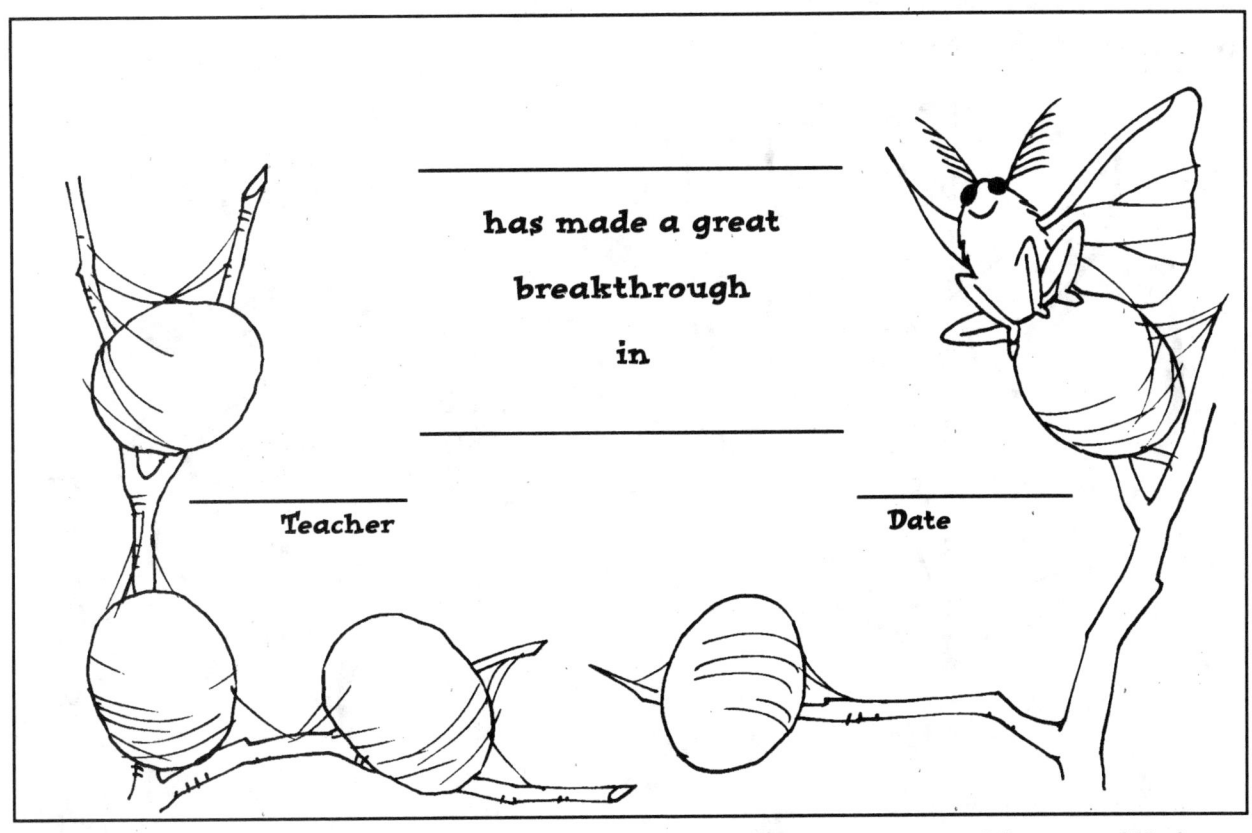

_____ is as Smooth As Silk when it comes to _____

_____ Teacher   _____ Date

_____ has made a great breakthrough in _____

_____ Teacher   _____ Date

Unit Management

Clip Art

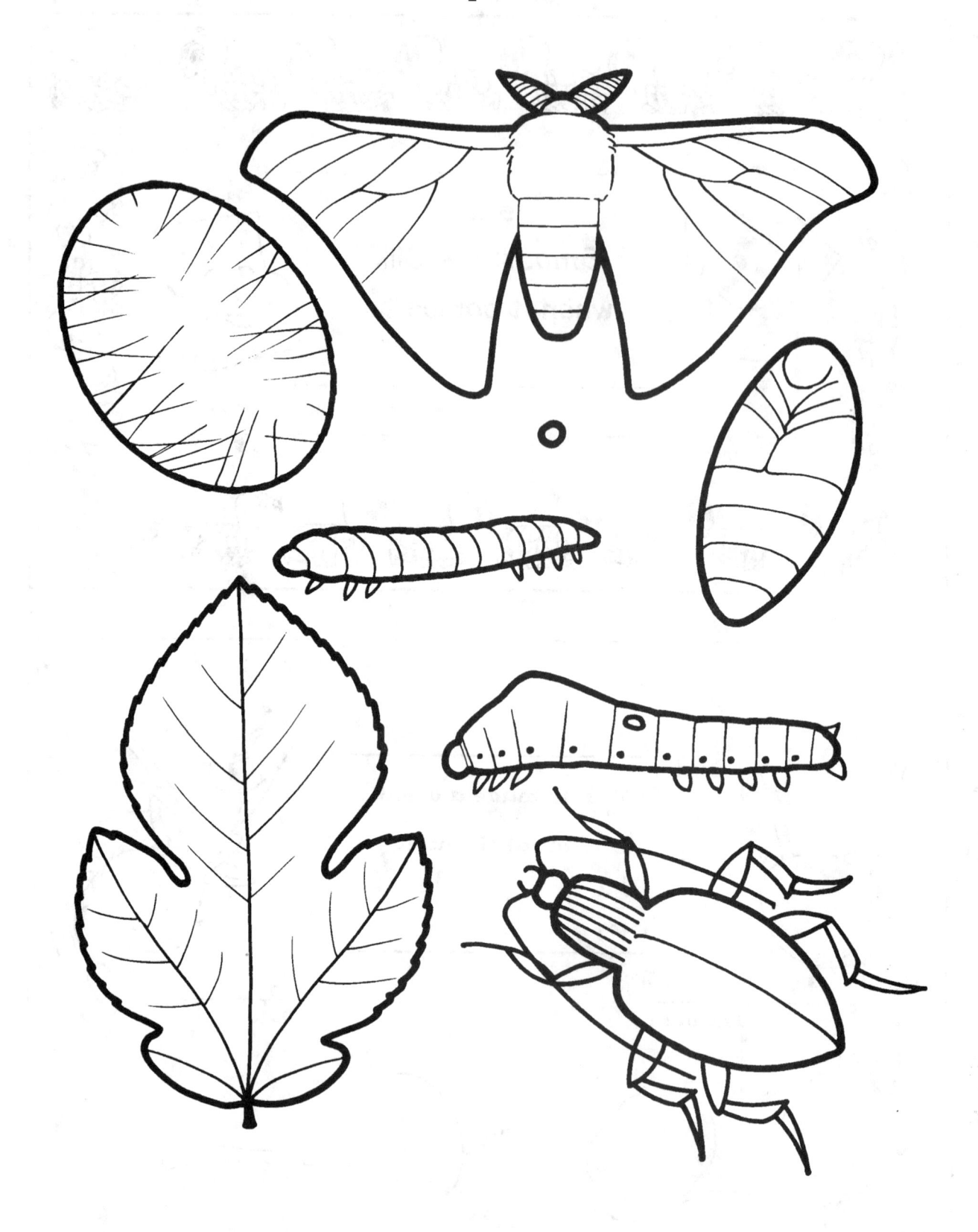

#2371 Thematic Unit—Silkworms and Mealworms © Teacher Created Materials, Inc.

Answer Key

Page 12—Domesticated Animals

silkworm, horse, cow, cat

Page 13—Metamorphosis Cycle

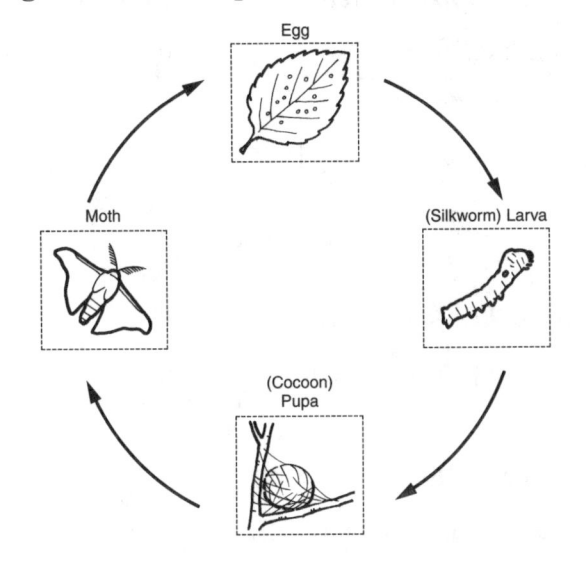

Egg → (Silkworm) Larva → (Cocoon) Pupa → Moth → Egg

Page 14—Unscramble Words

1. leaf
2. silk
3. moth
4. cocoon
5. larva
6. molt
7. antennae
8. pupa
9. egg

Page 20—Story Sequence

1. Teapot with cup and mooncakes.
2. Cocoon splashes into teacup.
3. Empress unraveling cocoon.
4. Servant unwinding cocoons.
5. Women sewing the new robe.
6. Emperor happy in silk robe.

Page 22—Compounded Animals

silkworm goldfish ladybug
butterfly mealworm bluebird

Page 23—Silkworm Search

1. Silkworms like to eat Mulberry leaves.
2. Silkworms are the larva of a moth.
3. A silkworm spins its cocoon out of silk.

Page 42—A Mealworm's Favorite Color

The mealworms will prefer the darker colors.

Page 51—Place Value Practice

1. 32   2. 50   3. 25
4. 42   5. 44   6. 19

Page 52—Mealworm Mania

1. 7   5. 8   9. 8
2. 8   6. 6   10. 5
3. 6   7. 7
4. 5   8. 7

Challenge: 15 shoes

Page 54—What am I? Riddles

1. silkworm moth   5. egg
2. simple eye   6. pupa
3. larva   7. spinneret
4. Mulberry leaf   8. cocoon

Page 59—Ways Insects Help Us

Helpful	Harmful
bee	grasshopper
butterfly	bee
ladybug	fly
worm	ant
silkworm	

(*Some creepy crawlies may fit in the Both column; it is rather subjective.*)

Page 68—Show What You Know

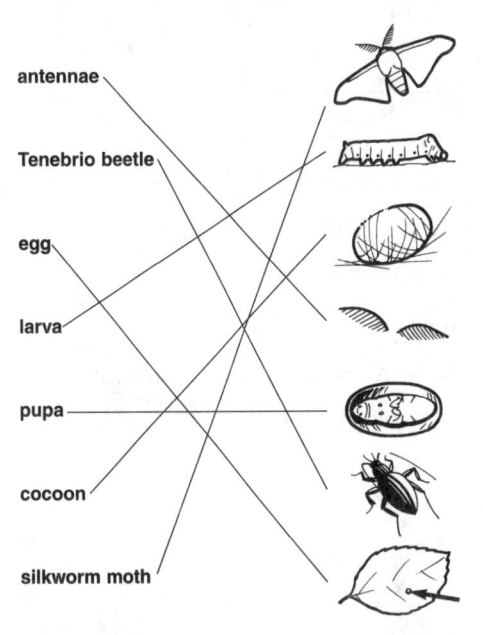

antennae — silkworm moth
Tenebrio beetle — larva
egg — pupa
larva — cocoon
pupa — egg
cocoon — beetle
silkworm moth — leaf

Bibliography

Arnett, R. H., and R.L. Jacques. *Insect Life: A Field Entomology Manual for the Amateur Naturalist*. Prentice Hall, 1985.

Coldrey, Jennifer. *Discovering Worms*. New York: Bookwright Press, 1986.

Coldrey, Jennifer. *The Silkworm Story*. London, 1983.

Coleman, Graham. *Worms (The New Creepy Crawly Collection)*. Gareth Stevens, July 1996.

Dineen, Jacqueline. *Cotton and Silk*. Enslow Publishers, Inc.,1988.

Fowler, Allan. *It Could Still be a Worm*. Children's Press, 1996.

Hong, Lily Toy. *The Empress and the Silkworm*. Albert Whitman & Co., 1995.

Johnson, Sylvia. *Silkworms*. First Avenue Editions, 1989.

Johnson, Sylvia. *Beetles*. Lerner Publications, Co., 1982.

Levy, Constance. *I'm Going to Pet a Worm Today; And Other Poems*. McElderry, 1991.

Miller, Billie. *Soo Ling: The Story of the Silkworm*. Kidship Association, 1991.

Oram, Hiawyn. *Creepy Crawly Song Book*. FS & G, 1993.

Royston, Angela. *Insects and Crawly Creatures*. Macmillan, 1992.

Stepp, Ann. *A Silkworm is Born*. New York, Sterling Publishing Company, 1972.

Still, John. *Amazing Butterflies and Moths*. Knopf, 1991.

Watts, Barrie. *Moths*. Silver Burdett Press, 1991.

Business Addresses

Insect Lore Box 1535 Shafter, CA 93263 1-800-LIVE-BUG
Fax: (805)-746-0334
Email: insect@lightspeed.net
Internet Address: http://www.insectlore.com

L'eggs Products (Pantyhose) P.O. Box 450 Winston-Salem, NC 27102   Phone: 1-800-92-LEGGS

Internet Addresses

Silkworms
http://www.cambodia.org/clubs/khemara/mulberry.htm
http://www.worldbutterfly.com
http://www.wnn.com/eggsilk.html

Mealworms
http://www.pythons.com/jurassic/html
http://www.mayhillpress.com/insects.html